PREACHING the HARD SAYINGS of JESUS

PREACHING

the

HARD SAYINGS

of

JESUS

JOHN T. CARROLL

JAMES R. CARROLL

© 1996 by Hendrickson Publishers, Inc.
P. O. Box 3473
Peabody, Massachusetts 01961–3473
Printed in the United States of America

ISBN 1–56563–230–3

First Printing — October 1996

Chapter 1 incorporates and adapts material first published in an article by John T. Carroll in *Biblical Literacy Today* (vol. 8, no. 3 [1994]); reprinted here by permission of the publisher.

Library of Congress Cataloging-in-Publication Data

Carroll, John T., 1954–
    Preaching the hard sayings of Jesus / by John T. Carroll
and James R. Carroll.
    Includes bibliographic references and indexes.
    ISBN 1–56563–230–3 (paper)
    1. Bible. N.T. Gospels—Homiletical use. 2. Jesus Christ—
Words. I. Carroll, James R. II. Title.
    BT306.C36   1997
    226´.06–dc20   96–15771
                                                                CIP

Cover art: Jesus drives out merchants from the Temple in this fresco by Giotto from the Scrovegni Chapel, Padua, Italy. Used with permission, Alinari/Art Resource, N.Y.

Cover design: Christopher Tobias/Tobias Designs

TABLE OF CONTENTS

PREFACE

FOR MANY WHO PICK UP THIS BOOK, THE TERRITORY WE SURVEY—THE teaching of Jesus of Nazareth—may seem familiar and well-charted. If we look closely, however, the terrain often turns out to be far more precarious than we had realized. Some of the sayings of Jesus are puzzling, others disconcerting or even disturbing. What, for example, are we to do with talk of hating parents or cutting off one's hand or foot? Naturally, we prefer to avoid such remarks. Yet when the church in its preaching and teaching steers clear of the hard sayings of Jesus, something of the genius and passion of Jesus is lost to us. And when we dutifully read but in the process seek to dull the cutting edge of these sayings, we are left with a domesticated Jesus who may be easier to live with but who can no longer claim life for the realm of God. The prophetic voice which might inspire, challenge, and invigorate us has then fallen silent.

We have written this book to help our readers come to terms with many of the most challenging words of Jesus. We have divided our labors along the lines of our own experience, James as a Presbyterian pastor for more than fifty years, John as a biblical scholar. From John's pen come the translations of each passage studied and the sections of the book entitled "An Interpretation." James is the author of the sections called "From Text to Sermon."

The partnership that led to the writing of this book began some forty-one years ago, when James became the father of John. It is our hope that the fruit of our collaboration is a book that will challenge our readers to rediscover and interpret responsibly for our day the hard sayings of Jesus.

John T. Carroll and James R. Carroll
Thanksgiving Day 1995

⸎

I began to wrestle with the hard sayings of Jesus as a child, when I listened in fascination to my father's preaching Sunday after Sunday. What a delight and inspiration it has been, therefore, to plan, discuss, and write this book with a master preacher to whom I owe such a great debt. I am deeply grateful to my father/coauthor and to my mother Mildred, who have both given me unfailing encouragement and support, and whose wisdom, faith, and commitment to justice have shaped my own life in ways that are certainly reflected, if perhaps too dimly, in these pages.

This book repays in small measure, but with heartfelt appreciation, Hal Horan and Bob Pierce, two preachers whose earnest wrestling with the hard sayings of Jesus has in recent years stimulated my efforts to think through the meaning of these challenging words—and to respond to them faithfully and creatively. I have learned much from the members of adult classes in several congregations, and from students and colleagues at Louisiana State University and Union Theological Seminary in Virginia. Olen and Edna Wilson of my home church in Amarillo, Grady Hines of Baton Rouge, and Stu Irvine, Jerry Kennedy, and Pam Bartlett among many other friends at University Presbyterian Church, Baton Rouge, deserve a special word of thanks for the many ways in which they have taught and encouraged me. A sabbatical leave from Union Theological Seminary enabled me to finish work on the book, and President Louis Weeks has been especially supportive of the project. I gladly acknowledge the expert editorial assistance of Patrick Alexander and the rest of the staff at

Hendrickson Publishers, without whom this book would have remained only a dream. Finally, I thank Cindy, Andrew, and Anna, whose companionship from day to day makes of home a little piece of heaven.

J. T. C.

⚜

My sharing in the writing of this book has been a task of joy. Who wouldn't revel in the collaboration with a brilliant son whose experience as a former pastor and as a biblical scholar has guided and enlightened a father who for fifty years and more has wrestled with the hard sayings of Jesus?

I confess that for the earlier years of my pastoral ministry I took the route of avoiding some of the troublesome words of Jesus by picking and choosing sermon passages which seemed easier. In later years the use of the Common Lectionary brought me face to face with the challenges which we have explored in this book.

Any preacher knows how important it is to have patient and thoughtful listeners. I was fortunate in preaching to three congregations whose love and support encouraged me to step into the pulpit Sunday by Sunday: Chestnut Level, Pennsylvania; Central Church in Buffalo, New York; and First Church in Amarillo, Texas. My part in this book is in a sense a "Thank You" to them. I learned much from working with and listening to associates on the staff at Buffalo and Amarillo. I cherish their friendship.

For more than fifty years my wife Mildred has labored with me, listened to my sermons, made helpful suggestions, and been a homemaker par excellence. Her wise counsel is reflected in these pages. We are grateful for our three children—James, John, and Judy—who made life easier and more joyous by their growing up in our home and whose own families have brought us the delights of grandparenthood. With

John I am indebted to our editor and staff at Hendrickson Publishers for their expert assistance.

John and I hope and pray that our joint labors in this book may be of help to fellow and sister pastors, to lay people in Bible study groups, and to all who earnestly seek to discover the treasures in the words of Jesus.

J. R. C.

ABBREVIATIONS

I. GENERAL ABBREVIATIONS

BCE	Before the Common Era (BC)
CE	Common Era (AD)
cf.	*confer*, compare
ch(s).	chapter(s)
ed.	edition; editors (edited by)
e.g.	*exempli gratia*, for example
esp.	especially
ET	English Translation
i.e.	*id est*, that is
n(n).	note(s)
LXX	Septuagint (the Greek Old Testament)
MT	Masoretic Text (of the OT)
NT	New Testament
orig.	original
OT	Old Testament
par.	parallel passage(s) in (an)other gospel(s)
rev.	revised (by)
vol(s).	volume(s)
v(v).	verse(s)

II. ANCIENT LITERATURE

A. Biblical Books with the Apocrypha

Gen	Genesis
Exod	Exodus
Lev	Leviticus
Num	Numbers

Deut	Deuteronomy
Judg	Judges
1–2 Kgs	1–2 Kings
Job	Job
Ps(s)	Psalm(s)
Prov	Proverbs
Isa	Isaiah
Jer	Jeremiah
Hos	Hosea
Mic	Micah
Hab	Habakkuk
Zech	Zechariah
Mal	Malachi
Sir	Sirach (Ecclesiasticus)
Tob	Tobit
Matt	Matthew
Rom	Romans
1–2 Cor	1–2 Corinthians
Gal	Galatians
Eph	Ephesians
Phil	Philippians
Heb	Hebrews
Jas	James
1–2 Pet	1–2 Peter
Rev	Revelation

B. Early Christian Writings

| *Gos. Thom.* | *Gospel of Thomas* |

C. Dead Sea Scrolls

| 11QTemple | *Temple Scroll* from Qumran Cave 11 |
| CD | *Damascus Document* |

D. Other Early Jewish Authors and Writings

1 Enoch	*Ethiopic Enoch*
Ant.	Josephus, *Antiquities of the Jews*
Jub.	*Jubilees*
T. Levi	*Testament of Levi*
T. Reuben	*Testament of Reuben*

III. MODERN LITERATURE

AB	Anchor Bible
ABRL	The Anchor Bible Reference Library
ABD	*The Anchor Bible Dictionary* (6 vols.; ed. David Noel Freedman)
ATR	*Anglican Theological Review*
AUS	American University Studies
CBQ	*Catholic Biblical Quarterly*
ExpT	*Expository Times*
HBC	*Harper's Bible Commentary* (ed. James Luther Mays)
HBD	*Harper's Bible Dictionary* (ed. Paul J. Achtemeier)
HTR	*Harvard Theological Review*
IBC	Interpretation: A Bible Commentary for Teaching and Preaching
ICC	International Critical Commentary
Int	*Interpretation*
JAAR	*Journal of the American Academy of Religion*
JBL	*Journal of Biblical Literature*
LBC	Layman's Bible Commentary
LCBI	Literary Currents in Biblical Interpretation
LCL	Loeb Classical Library
LEC	Library of Early Christianity
KJV	King James Version
NCB	New Century Bible
NIGTC	New International Greek Testament Commentary
NovT	*Novum Testamentum*
NRSV	New Revised Standard Version
NTM	New Testament Message
NTS	*New Testament Studies*
NTT	New Testament Theology
OBS	Oxford Bible Series
OBT	Overtures to Biblical Theology
PC	Proclamation Commentaries
PNTC	Pelican New Testament Commentaries
PS	The Passion Series
RB	*Revue biblique*
RSV	Revised Standard Version
SP	Sacra Pagina
TI	Theological Inquiries
TPINTC	Trinity Press International New Testament Commentary

TR	Theology and Religion
TS	*Theological Studies*
WUNT	Wissenschaftliche Untersuchungen zum Neuen Testament
ZSNT	Zacchaeus Studies: New Testament

INTRODUCTION

JESUS OF NAZARETH WAS A PROVOCATIVE TEACHER. HE TOLD STORIES that turned conventional views of God and human society upside down. Many of his one-liners (aphorisms) were just as challenging. What his words pictured, his deeds enacted. The rule of God was pressing into the world, redrawing the maps of the human community. Jesus offered words and gestures of grace for persons on the margins of the community—the sick, women, children, and "sinners." Moreover, he dared to question the impeccable religious credentials of the "righteous." As a result his message often offended, his actions brought scandal. Small wonder that the verdict pronounced on his life by human authority was that, as a dangerous disturber of the social order, he must be eliminated. The road from the scandalous, expansive grace of God to a Roman cross was not, it turned out, a very long one.

If those outside his circle of committed followers found Jesus' ministry disturbing and even threatening, persons drawn to his side found his teaching just as unsettling. He set the claims of God's realm above the most sacred of duties and relationships. The call to discipleship meant that possessions, security, home, and even family itself were now dispensable.

Jesus disturbed his contemporaries with words and practices that pointed to the expansive, boundary-shattering graciousness of God. And he challenged those who would commit themselves to his cause to give up everything they held dear. We who hear these words today find them no less disturbing. And there is more. For example, many modern readers also stumble over stark images pointing to the reality of judgment.

Does the mercy of God not nullify such outmoded ideas of a vengeful deity?

These hard sayings of Jesus take us right to the heart of Jesus' message. Therefore, much as we might like to avoid such texts, we ignore them at our own peril. At the same time, we face at every turn potential danger from mishearing them. There are serious questions here, for any—whether in the first century or the twenty-first—who would answer Jesus' call to discipleship. The first three chapters of this book pursue such questions, exploring in turn the "scandal of grace," the "cost of grace" (demands of discipleship), and the "offense of judgment." These hard sayings of Jesus are not so much hard to understand as hard to accept. But other sayings of Jesus are difficult for modern readers to comprehend. So often the obstacle to understanding is the considerable linguistic and cultural distance that separates us from Jesus' own culture. Chapter 4 treats two parables—the "dishonest steward" (Luke 16:1–8) and "a friend's help at midnight" (Luke 11:5–8)—that exemplify this problem.

Perhaps most unsettling of all to many Christians today are those passages in which Jesus appears as an all too human figure—evidently mistaken about the future of the world, pleading with God to remove the cup of his suffering, and crying out in despair as he dies cut off from the divine presence. How can such sentiments be reconciled with Christian convictions that Jesus is "true God of true God"? Chapter 5 probes this interpretive challenge, the scandal of Jesus' humanness.

APPROACH OF THE STUDY

In presenting our approach in this study, it may be well to indicate what the book is *not*. We do not pretend, first of all, to offer a comprehensive discussion of the teaching and preaching of Jesus, or even of the difficult sayings of Jesus. Rather than say a little about many passages, we have chosen instead to focus on a few especially important themes in Jesus' teaching, and to probe them at considerable depth.[1] Our interest is above all in elusive sayings that bewilder, trouble, and even offend the reader's sensibilities. As noted above, we organize the discussion around themes which we take to be pivotal in Jesus' work and message. In doing so, of course, we must take care not to impose on the sayings an interpretive grid that is contrived and distorts meaning. The advantage of our thematic arrangement is that it will help to focus attention on crucial features of Jesus' ministry.

Second, ambitious as our project is (these are, after all, *hard* sayings!), we have not undertaken an even more difficult task, the construction of the historical career and message of Jesus. That is, we do not attempt to reconstruct in precise detail the original form and content of these words of Jesus, sifted from the layers of interpretation that have reshaped them as they continued to speak, in early Christian memory, to the problems and needs of the earliest Christian communities.[2] Yet, on the whole, it is reasonable to claim that these hard sayings do in fact confront us with the voice of Jesus. For it is precisely these words that set Jesus apart from other teachers of his day; these words that posed such an interpretive challenge to the earliest Christians who kept retelling them to each new generation.[3] At the end of the day, then, we will find that we have indeed been wrestling with the hard sayings *of Jesus.*

Third, we do not in these pages present a thorough treatment of the sayings of Jesus in relation to their narrative contexts within the gospels.[4] We do recognize and affirm the importance and value of literary study of the gospels which insists that each saying be read as a part of the narrative in which it is embedded. Indeed, we will often build an interpretation or homiletical application of a text on this kind of narrative analysis. It is important to realize, however, that the narrative contexts in which these sayings of Jesus now appear were not the original settings in which he spoke them. Early Christian memory of Jesus' teaching did not preserve those generative contexts with any precision, as a glance at the gospels plainly shows. Matthew's "sermon on the mount" (Matt 5–7), for example, draws together teachings of Jesus that are distributed throughout Luke and in quite different settings. Some of this material corresponds to Luke's "sermon on the plain" (Luke 6), but much appears elsewhere in Luke. Notably, the prayer taught by Jesus to his disciples (the "Lord's Prayer") is placed by Matthew within the sermon on the mount (6:9–13), while in Luke (in a shorter form) it responds to a specific request from the disciples (Luke 11:2–4). And where did Jesus speak the words assembled in the lengthy discourse on "last things" (Mark 13; Matt 24–25; Luke 21:5–36; cf. Luke 17:22–37)? Both Mark and Matthew locate this teaching on the Mount of Olives, although Mark restricts the audience of disciples to Peter, James, John, and Andrew (Mark 13:3; cf. Matt 24:3). Luke, though, presents these words as part of Jesus' public teaching within the temple (see Luke 20:45; 21:37). The examples could be multiplied, but perhaps the point is clear enough. Words receive meaning in the particular contexts in which they are spoken, but we do not know in precise detail the specific contexts which first called forth the hard sayings of Jesus.

We can suggest in a tentative way, however, the general circumstance or feature of Jesus' work that makes sense of a particular saying. And sometimes these inferences drawn from the saying itself may square rather well with the narrative setting provided by the gospel author. So, for example, the parable of the "prodigal son" (see ch. 1 below) does appear to lend legitimacy to Jesus' acceptance of "sinners," as Luke 15:1–2 already intimates. But the point we are making is that when we interpret these hard sayings, it is sometimes helpful to listen to the saying on its own terms, independent of the narrative setting provided by the gospel writer. There is a value in trying to recapture the original social and cultural setting to which the words spoke, as distinct from the later social and cultural worlds of, say, Luke or Matthew.

In the pages that follow we will be doing both kinds of analysis. From time to time we will try to hear in a parable an echo of the message first articulated by Jesus, a message obscured somewhat by later retellings.[5] But we will in other cases be guided by the clues to meaning left by the place the saying has been given in the gospel narrative. The creative work of the preacher and teacher can receive a stimulus, we think, from both ways of approaching these texts.

Fourth, we do not presume to offer any definitive interpretations of the texts we explore. Such an aim would be neither possible nor desirable, for so many sayings of Jesus resist reduction to a single meaning. This is especially true of the parables, which by their very design evoke divergent interpretations and responses from different hearers. Yet as we grapple earnestly with the challenging words of Jesus, we do hope to stimulate the creative thought and reflection of our readers as they take up the challenging task of appropriating these sayings for our common life today.

For each of the sayings that we treat, readers will find an original translation, an interpretation that addresses pivotal exegetical issues, reflections on the passage framed with a view to homiletical appropriation, and suggestions for further reading. The coauthors have endeavored to keep the "interpretation" and the "proclamation" in close conversation throughout the study. Nevertheless, we have not always heard or responded to these hard sayings in exactly the same way. We have chosen to refrain from suppressing all interpretive differences between us, even as our thinking has consistently moved in the same general direction. We leave it to our readers to adjudicate any creative tensions that remain.

ENDNOTES

[1] For brief treatments of a wider range of texts, one may consult, e.g., F. F. Bruce, *The Hard Sayings of Jesus* (Downers Grove, Ill.: InterVarsity, 1983).

[2] An elegant statement of the problem may be found in Günther Bornkamm, *Jesus of Nazareth* (San Francisco: Harper & Row, 1960) 13–26.

[3] In other words, application of the criterion or test of *dissimilarity* supports the claim that these sayings actually come from Jesus rather than from other teachers contemporaneous with him or from later Christian prophets and teachers.

[4] For an excellent discussion of the parables within their narrative contexts in the gospels, see John R. Donahue, *The Gospel in Parable* (Philadelphia: Fortress, 1988).

[5] A stimulating treatment of the parables in this vein is that of Bernard Brandon Scott, *Hear Then the Parable* (Minneapolis: Fortress, 1989).

THE SCANDAL OF GRACE

Look, a glutton and a drunkard, a friend
of tax collectors and sinners! (Luke 7:34)

G RACE, IN THE HANDS OF JESUS, IS DIFFICULT TO ACCEPT. IT IS NO
respecter of conventional social boundaries. His stories
and his meals and his healings betray a decided preference for
the socially marginal, for the religiously unrespectable. Indeed,
Luke records Jesus' own admission that, in the eyes of his
critics, he was nothing other than a "friend of tax collectors
and sinners." In a word, in the message and public ministry of
Jesus grace is offensive, even scandalous. In this chapter we
explore several sayings of Jesus which provoke the hearer with
their celebration of the offense of divine grace.

THE "GOOD SAMARITAN":
REIMAGING AN ENEMY (LUKE 10:30–35)

Translation

> *A certain man was going down from Jerusalem to Jericho and fell*
> *into the hands of robbers, who after stripping and beating him went*
> *away, leaving him half-dead. Now by chance a certain priest was*
> *going down on that road, and when he saw him he passed by on the*
> *other side. In the same way also, when a Levite came to the place*
> *and saw [him], he passed by on the other side. But a certain*
> *Samaritan on a journey approached him, and when he saw he was*
> *moved to pity, and coming up he bound his wounds, pouring on*

[them] olive oil and wine; and he set him on his own animal and brought him to an inn and took care of him. And on the next day he took out two denarii and gave them to the innkeeper; and he said, "Take care of him, and whatever more you spend, I will repay you when I return."

An Interpretation

The story about an anonymous man robbed and beaten on the dangerous road from Jerusalem to Jericho (Luke 10:30–35) is one of the best known of Jesus' parables. If we follow the clues left by Luke in his crafting of the narrative, we read the parable as an "example story" illustrating the "love of neighbor" emphasized in the preceding conversation (Luke 10:25–29).[1] By turning the question "who is my neighbor?" into the question "which [one] was a neighbor to the man who fell into the hands of the robbers?", the parable refuses to set any limits on the command to love. The Samaritan functions, then, as a model of Christian love. If a despised Samaritan can show love of neighbor in this way, certainly a Christian reader can do the same (v. 37: "Go and do likewise"). This interpretation of the parable has considerable force; after all, it appears to be the way Luke read the parable and wished his first readers to hear it; moreover, it can inspire a hard-hitting sermon motivating concrete acts of compassion toward those in need, no matter what their race, class, or nationality.[2]

But if we approach the parable with an eye to its setting within the ministry of Jesus himself (as distinct from the narrative setting Luke has provided), we may discover a particularly hard saying of Jesus. It is instructive to ask how the first audience of the story—Jesus' hearers—would have made sense of the parable. Would they have identified with the Samaritan as a positive role model? Or would they rather have identified with the nameless man in the ditch and reacted to the story's plot through his eyes? The story begins, "A certain man was going down from Jerusalem to Jericho." A Jewish listener would assume that the man was a fellow Jew, since he is not otherwise identified.[3] Particularly in light of the misfortunes that overtake the man, Jesus' hearer would identify with the man lying in the ditch. The parable entices us to view what happens through his eyes.

Two religious leaders happen upon the scene, one a priest and the other a Levite. It is possible that both are returning to Jericho, a town where many priests reside, after fulfilling their temple duties, but the parable does not say so. In any event, both men cross to the other side of the road, failing to assist the victim. The parable is silent concerning their motivation. Did they fear an ambush? Did they suppose the man was dead (the parable describes him as "half-dead") and so wish to avoid the ritual impurity which would accompany handling a corpse?[4] The parable's hearer can only guess, but that leaves the listener in exactly the same position as the man in the ditch. Whatever the reasons for their inaction, the priest and the Levite have failed to show compassion. Suspense builds: will help arrive in time?

With the failure of two priestly functionaries, one expects a Jewish layperson to appear.[5] The surprising twist the story now takes will not be lost on Jesus' listeners—indeed, it will offend them—and it also indicates that the point of the story is not an attack against the clergy. A Samaritan arrives on the scene—that is to say, a person whom victim and listener alike distrust, dislike, and despise. We can only expect the worst. So the story will end on a tragic note? Yet this Samaritan, of all people, shows compassion to the man in the ditch, to the point of paying for several days' rest and recuperation at an inn. Lying helpless, vulnerable, at the mercy of his enemy, the man must accept aid from even such a one. Loving an enemy is one thing; in that case one remains in control, one derives satisfaction from being unusually magnanimous.[6] But seeing oneself as vulnerable in the face of an enemy, and helped by him rather than by one's own kind, is disconcerting. The parable forces a hearer to reimage the enemy and so disturbs the order of a world where friends are friends and foes are foes.

The story of Jewish–Samaritan hostilities is a long one; we do not need to review it here.[7] Two somewhat later Jewish texts will serve to illustrate the disdain Jews felt for Samaritans, thus confirming the reading we have given the parable. Mishnah tractate *Šebiᶜit* 8.10 reflects the hostility of Jews toward the Samaritans: "One who eats bread [baked by] Samaritans is like one who eats pork."[8] And according to tractate *Sanhedrin* (57a) in the Babylonian Talmud (compiled in the fifth century CE), while a Samaritan guilty of murdering a Jew must be punished, the death penalty does not apply in the case of a Jew's murder of a Samaritan (Cuthean). Clearly, this parable about a "good Samaritan" challenges and overturns a deeply held rejection of Samaritans as outsiders. Victimized by bandits from one's own people, one is rescued by an enemy. The story affords a disturbing glimpse of the world, threatening to undo carefully cultivated distinctions between "us" and "them." It explodes the "cold war" mentality and presses beyond détente, beyond a peaceful, yet uneasy coexistence, to acceptance of the full humanity of the other and of the genuine good that lies within him or her. Divine grace can offend my religious sensibilities, for it sometimes comes from the most unexpected of sources, from a person I would rather hate. Now, Jesus has taken that option away from me!

From Text to Sermon: "Friend or Enemy?"

Familiarity can make us blind. I use the telephone many times a day. But don't ask me to draw a picture of the dial and put all the digits and letters in their proper places. What about traffic signals? We encounter scores of them every week. But is the red light or the green light at the top? I had read the parable of the "Good Samaritan" and the story of the rich ruler (Luke 18:18–25) countless times. But only after thirty years or so did I notice that these two—the parable and the story—begin with the same question: "What must I do to inherit eternal life?"

Yes, two different people ask Jesus the same question. One questioner is a lawyer, a student of Scripture. The other is a Jewish ruler. Jesus recognizes, in his conversations with both, that their theology is sound. Yet each has a problem with living out his faith, and that problem assumes a different shape for the two. Each therefore requires a different answer. The ruler, we learn, is a wealthy man (Mark's gospel describes him as a "young man"). He has a problem with *things*. Jesus tells him,

"Sell all that you own and distribute the money to the poor."
In other words, "Your problem is money." We can hear the
wealthy man respond, "Money a problem? Not for me. I have
plenty!" We can also hear the Master's answer: "Yes; but
money has plenty of you. You can't manage it. Money is
managing you."

The problem of the lawyer, on the other hand, is not
things, but *people!* To inherit eternal life one must be able to
accept and relate positively to people, all kinds of people.
Loving one's neighbor begins with the dimensions of the heart
and not the size of the neighborhood! The lawyer wants Jesus
to set boundaries to define "neighbor": race, religion, nationality. He wants Jesus to draw a circle around "neighbor."

It is time for a story! We call it "the parable of the good
Samaritan." A man—undoubtedly a Jewish brother—is traveling from Jerusalem to Jericho. He is beaten, robbed, and left
half dead. A priest and a Levite, in turn going down the road,
pass by on the other side. Perhaps questions like these cross
their minds: Is the victim a "brother"? Is he still alive? Can I
risk defilement? Can I risk involvement? Dare I take the time to
investigate? For the priest and the Levite, life is not *on* the road
but *at the end of* the road. (How much do we all miss because
we see the journey on the road not as part of life but as merely
the way to life at the journey's end?)

A shocking thing now takes place. A hated, heretical half-
breed—a Samaritan—stops, administers first aid, and on his
own beast of burden brings the victim to the nearest inn. He
makes provision for the man's care, room, and board. An
enemy sees his enemy as a fellow human being in need and
responds accordingly.

Jesus does not answer the lawyer's query, "And who is my
neighbor?" For the lawyer has asked the wrong question. At the
end of the parable Jesus poses the right question: "Which one
was a neighbor?" Boundaries and barriers disappear! The question of "neighbor," we discover, begins in the heart, not in the
hinterland of one's likes and dislikes, peeves and prejudices.
Christ calls us to *be* neighbors rather than merely to *have*
neighbors. Christian love does not pick and choose.

He drew a circle that shut me out—
Heretic, rebel, a thing to flout.
But love and I had the wit to win:
We drew a circle that took him in.[9]

One does not draw the line between friend and enemy, white and black, American and Russian, Muslim and Christian, Arab and Jew, poor and rich, Presbyterian and Roman Catholic. We in the United States some fifty years ago regarded Germany and Japan as our enemies. Now we count them as friends. The change occurred because, among other things, we decided to be neighborly. Just a few years ago, who would have dared to hope that the wall dividing East and West Germany would finally be torn down? And who would have thought that the heads of the Palestine Liberation Organization and of the state of Israel would shake hands—in a courageous gesture of mutual respect and commitment to the precarious task of peacemaking? Enmity can give way to friendship, animosity to respect, distrust to trust. But such change requires persons of vision, persons of faith who will take the risk of being neighbor to an enemy. Let that miracle take place in Sarajevo, in Northern Ireland, in Beirut, in Tel Aviv, in Baghdad, in Washington, and in my own hometown, my own church.

Several years ago, I had the privilege of attending the General Assembly of the Cumberland Presbyterian Church in San Antonio and extending greetings from our sister denomination (United Presbyterian Church U.S.A.). I forget what I said. I still remember, though, what the moderator of the Second Cumberland Church (predominantly African American) said in his message to the same Assembly. He spoke of how the time long since had come when the two denominations (Cumberland and Second Cumberland) should unite. He said, "We have churches in the same towns, on the same streets, and on the same street corners. Our trouble is: we are close enough together, but we are too far apart!" What he said could have applied not long ago to more than one hundred years of separation between the "northern" and "southern" branches of the Presbyterian Church in the United States.

The victims of prejudice, injustice, and violence are waiting for a "good Samaritan." I need grace—grace to accept an enemy's kindness, grace to love a stranger, an enemy. God help me to be a neighbor.

For Further Reading

Ronald J. Allen, in *Preaching Biblically: Creating Sermons in the Shape of Scripture* (ed. Don M. Wardlaw; Philadelphia: Westminster, 1983) 39–56.

James Breech, *The Silence of Jesus: The Authentic Voice of the Historical Man* (Philadelphia: Fortress, 1983) 158–83.

Fitzmyer, *Gospel according to Luke*, 2.882–90.

Jan Lambrecht, *Once More Astonished: The Parables of Jesus* (New York: Crossroad, 1981) 57–84.

Pheme Perkins, *Hearing the Parables of Jesus* (New York: Paulist, 1981) 112–23.

Scott, *Hear Then the Parable*, 189–202.

THE PHARISEE AND THE TAX COLLECTOR AT PRAYER: THE SCANDAL OF GRACE FOR SINNERS (LUKE 18:10–14a)

Translation

Two men went up to the temple to pray, the one a Pharisee and the other a tax collector. The Pharisee, standing by himself,[10] prayed these [words]: "God, I thank you that I am not like other human beings—robbers, swindlers, adulterers—or even like this tax collector. I fast twice a week; I pay a tithe [on] everything that I buy." But the tax collector, standing far off, did not wish even to raise his eyes toward heaven; rather, he was beating his breast, saying: "God, be merciful to me, a sinner." I tell you, this man—not the other—went down to his home vindicated.

An Interpretation

Beyond a doubt, Pharisees are the villains in the gospel accounts of Jesus' public ministry. They appear as self-righteous, greedy, envious, and hypocritical. An occasional exception does not affect this dominant image of the Pharisees left by the gospels. Because of this characterization of the Pharisees, which modern readers are inclined to accept at face value as part of the interpretive apparatus they have inherited, Jesus' story about a Pharisee and a tax collector at prayer often goes unrecognized for the hard saying it truly is. Hearers today applaud this deserved reproof of a self-righteous, pompous Pharisee. And indeed, Luke tells the story to make precisely that point. In introducing the parable (18:9), he offers his own editorial comment: "He also told this parable to some who trusted in themselves that they were righteous and regarded others with contempt." Moreover, Luke clinches the parable's point by adding, at the end, a saying of Jesus about role reversal: "for all who exalt themselves will be humbled, but all who humble themselves will be exalted" (v. 14).[11]

But would Jesus and his listeners have heard the story in this way? It is crucial to recognize that the gospel portrayals of the Pharisees are caricatures, shaped to a great extent by conflict between the first generations of Christian Jews (after Jesus' death and resurrection) and their non-Christian fellow Jews. After the destruction of the temple and the crushing defeat suffered by Jerusalem at the hands of Rome in 70 CE, it was the Pharisees and their heirs who would emerge as architects of the future of Judaism. Other influential Jewish groups from the pre-war period lost influence and ultimately disappeared from the scene altogether. As a result, when early Christians experienced conflict with Jews, whether it occurred within the synagogue between Christian and non-Christian Jews, or between the synagogue and Christians (Jewish or gentile), it was increasingly conflict with a rabbinic Judaism which preserved the traditions of the Pharisees of Jesus' day. Small wonder, then, that the gospel writers, in narrating Jesus' public ministry, told the story in light of the sometimes heated controversies of a later day. As generally happens in such controversies, caricatures took the place of accurate characterizations of one's opponents. It is imperative that the modern interpreter of Jesus' teaching recognize this process through which the life and teaching of Jesus were refracted in the last half of the first century CE.[12]

As we have seen, Luke presents this parable about a Pharisee and a tax collector at prayer as a rebuke of self-righteous-
ness that despises others as less worthy than oneself. Yet, for
Jesus' first hearers, the Pharisee in this story, far from being the
epitome of a false piety corrupted by self-righteous pride,
would have represented a model of piety and virtue worthy of
their emulation. The Pharisee offers a prayer of thanksgiving
for the exemplary life God has enabled him to live.[13] He has
gone far beyond what the Torah requires, fasting twice weekly[14]
and showing himself so scrupulous in tithing that he pays the
tithe even on items he purchases (even though the seller likely
would already have paid a tithe on them). But everything rides
on the comparison the Pharisee's prayer now draws between
himself and "this tax collector." Thank God I am not like him!

Of course, he is right. Jewish tax collectors in the time of
Jesus were regarded, with reason, as sinners, whose conduct
was antithetical to God's Torah. They were notorious for over-
charging their fellow Jews, in order to ensure collection of the
requisite taxes for payment to the local governing authority.[15] A
job entailing such risks (and earning such contempt) surely
warranted profit-taking as well. Not only did these tax collectors accumulate their wealth at the expense of their fellow Jews,
but also, in the process, they made themselves perpetually
"unclean" through their contact with gentiles and gentile coin.
Evidently, the tax collector of Jesus' parable was no different
from "the rest," for in his prayer he acknowledges the sad truth:
"God, be merciful to me, a sinner." The man knows full well
that he has no business being in this place of holiness, symbolic
of the divine presence. His halting plea for mercy accompanies
body language that is equally revealing. Beating his breast in
remorse, he cannot even bring himself to lift his eyes toward
heaven (the conventional posture of prayer). The Pharisee's
prayer of thanksgiving is justified. Thank God I am not like
him. Thank God the world has good, upright, responsible,
obedient people alongside others who respect neither law nor
fellow human being.

And yet . . . and yet it is just this contrast between righteous Pharisee and unrighteous tax collector, assuming (appro-

priately enough) the moral and religious superiority of the Pharisee, that is the crux of the parable. Something has gone wrong here, where the good man claims—even as he gives credit to God for the moral chasm that separates him from the tax collector—to stand in the favor of God while the other does not. The parable does not expose the hypocrisy or rebuke the arrogance of a self-righteous Pharisee. Its edge is much sharper than that. Instead, it calls into question the apparently reasonable belief that God's gracious presence honors obedient piety while scorning those whose lives have been marked by disobedience. In fact, God's response to these two prayers surprises the hearer, for the self-admitted sinner, not the virtuous man, is said to return home *dedikaiomenos,* that is, vindicated, acquitted, in the right [with God]. Small wonder, indeed, that the one who told this story earned the rebuke: "a friend of tax collectors and sinners!"

The scandal of grace, as expressed in this story of two men at prayer, is that the righteous stand no closer to God than do those among the unrighteous who recognize the divine presence for what it is—a holiness that puts to shame all human deeds laying claim to divine grace. The initiative of grace lies with God, and in its freedom to embrace a sinner—perhaps even over the objections of an exemplary individual—it shatters the expectations of human beings who prefer to structure their social world into polarities of good and bad, holy and unholy, pious and godless.

From Text to Sermon: "Overheard at a Prayer Meeting"

The author of the Letter of James writes, "The prayer of a righteous man has great power in its effects" (5:16 RSV). But Jesus told a parable in which the prayer of an evidently righteous man effected only his own judgment. Why? It appears that, for Jesus, there is a righteousness that shuts off life from grace. We call the story the parable of the Pharisee and the publican (tax collector) at prayer. According to Luke, Jesus' audience was a group of people "who trusted in themselves that they were righteous and regarded others with contempt."

An old African-American spiritual celebrates the fact that in heaven slaves, who were barefoot on earth, and all God's other "chill'un" would have shoes. But the same song reminds us that some of those who talk about heaven "ain't goin' there." In Jesus' parable a Pharisee—one of religion's elite—took for granted that he would be in the vanguard of the heavenly parade. In his prayer the Pharisee thanked God that he was not like other people. And isn't the world a better place because of good, dedicated persons like this Pharisee? Yet, even as he gave credit to God for his exemplary life, he patted himself on the back. He had no rival in self-esteem; no one could love him more than he loved himself. He was like Edith in a novelist's description: Edith was surrounded on east, west, north, and south by Edith!

As the Pharisee prayed he saw out of the corner of his eye a publican also at prayer. Probably he was amazed to see a despised tax collector praying. For tax collectors in an occupied land were collaborators with the enemy. They were betrayers of their own people. The Pharisee thanked God that he was not like that publican. Perhaps he thought: How dare that man use God's name in prayer? Or presume to darken the door of the temple? "Twice a week," the Pharisee continued, "I fast. Every shekel I tithe."

But as the proud man, standing off by himself, prayed in this way, the publican with down-turned eyes prayed, "God, be merciful to me, a sinner!"

Would God hear the prayer of such a man as this? Jesus surprises us with his picture of God's response to this prayer. The flood gates of heaven open wide, and this social and religious outcast's life begins to overflow with grace. Jesus said, "I tell you, this man, rather than the other, went down to his home justified."

Before we throw stones at the Pharisee, whom Jesus unmasks as blameworthy even in his righteous prayer, let us ask where we nourish our own pride. A church school teacher was once telling this parable to the girls and boys in his class. When he had finished, he said, "Now, let us bow our heads and thank God we are not like the Pharisee!" (We chuckle because we think we are not like the church school teacher!)

While I was serving a church in Buffalo, New York, our custodian each week placed a quote or saying on the bulletin board in front of the building. One week he had the line, "This church is for sinners only." Later that week I received in the mail an anonymous letter which went like this: "I am shocked to learn that our church is for sinners only. I've been a member of this church for twenty-five years, and I never realized that I was out of place and not welcome." When I showed the letter to the custodian, we agreed on a quote for the following week. It came from Romans 3:23: "All have sinned and fall short of the glory of God."

The parable about two men at prayer underscores the scandal of grace for sinners. Humility is the great equalizer. Pride separates a person from other human beings and from God. At the cross, all stand or kneel on the same level. No pedestals or high horses or step ladders are available to accommodate proud Pharisees or pompous Presbyterians.

This parable is for preachers, too. Those of us who proclaim the Word from the pulpit are susceptible to grandiose illusions. A parishioner once said to the preacher as he left the worship service on Sunday morning: "Pastor, did you know that was a great sermon you preached today?" "Yes," the minister replied, "the devil whispered that to me just as I stepped out of the pulpit!"

According to Luke, Jesus told the parable to those "who trusted in themselves that they were righteous and regarded others with contempt." God forbid that our attitudes or our conduct—even in our goodness, our righteousness—should be destructive, like the prayer of that righteous Pharisee. What do others see? Citizens of the United States alienating Canadians and Mexicans because we think we are better? Homeowners looking down at the homeless because they are shiftless and lazy? Those on diets to keep trim or get thin belittling the hungry because they go through the trash to keep alive?

The offense of grace! "Truly I tell you," Jesus said on one occasion, "the tax collectors and the prostitutes are going into the kingdom of God ahead of you" (Matt 21:31). Does such a word make us angry? Let us then be angry . . . until we are ashamed. Finally, even if we are righteous Pharisees, we shall pray, in all sincerity, with the publican: "God, be merciful to me, a sinner!" And then we shall be saved. But only then!

For Further Reading

Donahue, *Gospel in Parable*, 187–93.
Fitzmyer, *Gospel according to Luke*, 2.1182–90.
Joachim Jeremias, *Rediscovering the Parables* (New York: Scribner's, 1966) 111–15.
Jürgen Moltmann, in *A Chorus of Witnesses: Model Sermons for Today's Preacher* (ed. Thomas G. Long and Cornelius Plantinga Jr.; Grand Rapids: Eerdmans, 1994) 21–33.
Perkins, *Hearing the Parables of Jesus*, 171–76.
Eduard Schweizer, *The Good News according to Luke* (Atlanta: John Knox, 1984) 280–84.
Scott, *Hear Then the Parable*, 93–97.

ALL IN A DAY'S (OR AN HOUR'S?) WORK:
WHEN GRACE IS NOT FAIR (MATT 20:1–15)

Translation

> [There was once] a man, a householder, who went out early in the morning to hire laborers for his vineyard. And when he had agreed with the workers on a denarius for the day, he sent them into his vineyard. And as he went out at about the third hour,[16] he saw others standing in the marketplace idle. He said to those men, "You, too, go into the vineyard, and I will pay you whatever is right." So they went. At about the sixth hour and at about the ninth hour he went out again and did the same thing. Now when he went out at about the eleventh hour, he found others standing [around], and he says[17] to them, "Why have you stood here idle all day?" They tell him, "Because nobody hired us." He says to them, "You, too, go into the vineyard."
>
> Now when evening came, the owner of the vineyard says to his foreman, "Call the workers and pay them their wages, beginning with the last and on up to the first [hired]."[18] And when those who [had been hired] at about the eleventh hour came, they received a

*denarius apiece. So when the first came, they thought they would
receive more. Yet they, too, received a denarius apiece. As they took
[the money], they were complaining against the householder, saying, "These last worked one hour, and you have made them equal to
us, who have borne the burden of the day and the scorching heat."
But he replied to one of them, "Friend, I am doing you no wrong.
Didn't you agree with me for a denarius? Take what is yours and
go. (Nevertheless, I want to give to this last one just as [I gave] you.
Am I not allowed to do what I want with what belongs to me? Or is
your eye evil because I am good?)"*[19]

An Interpretation

Jesus' parable about two men at prayer may well provoke
the protest, "But that's not fair!" This protest, now articulated
for the listener by characters in the parable, is the crux of the
story of the vineyard workers, all of whom receive the same
wages although some have worked all day while others have
labored for only one hour.

This story must have struck Jesus' first listeners as especially true-to-life. It presupposes the hard facts of life known to
first century Palestinian Jews (and to many people of the
twentieth century as well): high unemployment, exhausting
labor for a subsistence wage (for those fortunate enough to
secure work), and the considerable power wielded by a landowner over both his land and his hired workers. "Am I not
allowed to do what I want with what belongs to me?" Indeed.
Yet, this is not a tale about a capricious, wealthy landowner who
drives a hard bargain. The owner surprises with his unpre-
dictable behavior, to be sure, but his caprice benefits rather
than harms, defying the expectations of others in the direction
not of hard-heartedness but of compassion.

The parable is laden with suspense. While an explicit
contract was formulated in the case of the workers first hired
("at a denarius for the day"), we do not know how much those
hired later will receive. As they go to their labors in the vineyard, they can only trust in the fairness of the owner, who
pledged to give them "whatever is *dikaion* (just, right)."[20] And
here is the surprise. Although the vineyard owner does not
show himself to be unreservedly generous and holds to the

original terms of the agreement reached with his all-day workers, he does display a measure of generosity when he insists on giving the same amount to laborers who worked only part of the day, even and especially to those whose one hour of toil was lightened by the first cool breeze of early evening. In the owner's eyes, that is the fair amount.[21] In the eyes of the full-day laborers, however, this is not at all fair.

The point of the parable is not, as many interpreters have suggested, the abundant grace or generosity of the vineyard owner.[22] One denarius for a day's hard labor would represent a subsistence wage, appropriate to the social and economic norms of the day, but certainly not an abundantly generous wage. Nor does the accent fall on the exclusion of the grumbling, full-day workers from grace, as if the owner's dismissal of them, with their wages, at the story's end meant that they were departing forever from his gracious presence.[23] No, the crux of the story is the contrast between these two groups, one earning their just wage, the other receiving it as an undeserved gift. As the tax collector at prayer received surprising vindication from God, despite his unworthiness, so too here the one-hour workers are awarded a full day's pay, despite their failure to earn it.[24] The challenge posed by both parables is the demand they make of the hearer to recognize and to accept God's embrace of the less deserving. This appeal will gain in dramatic urgency in the parable of the "prodigal son."

The parable of the vineyard workers leaves the angry laborers with a question, and since we hearers have identified with those workers in their outrage at an instance of evident injustice, the story leaves the same haunting question with us as well. "Is your eye evil because I am good?" We might paraphrase: Are you so tied to an egocentric vision that you discern in my gesture of kindness to another only an act willfully depreciating you? Therefore, like the parable of the Pharisee and the tax collector at prayer, and like the parable of the "prodigal son," as we will soon see, this story appeals to its hearer to accept God's scandalous embrace of those who are undeserving. God's grace scandalizes; in our concern for justice will we fail to recognize divine presence? (The vineyard, of course, is a long-standing metaphor for Israel, the people of divine promise and divine presence.)[25] With this parable, then, Jesus may be responding to the anger his own acceptance of the unrighteous has kindled among the righteous.[26] The story summons modern hearers to respond to that same surprising grace. Are we able to perceive divine presence even when, in its acknowledgment of the unworthy, it appears to contradict the conventional calculus of right and justice in human society?

From Text to Sermon: "Grace Is Not a Fair-minded Lady!"

W. A. B. Martin wrote a little book entitled *Grace Is Not a Blue-eyed Blonde.* We may title a sermon about the parable of the vineyard workers "Grace Is Not a Fair-minded Lady." For once again, as in the parable of the good Samaritan and the parable of the Pharisee and the publican at prayer, we are tempted to protest the offensive, even scandalous nature of God's grace. The parable of the good Samaritan pictures neighborly love coming from an enemy. The parable of the Pharisee and the publican at prayer pictures the grace of acceptance offered not because of the devotion of a good man but because of the confession of sin by a notorious sinner. The parable of the vineyard workers paints a shocking scene in which day laborers who put in one hour get paid the same wage as workers who put in twelve hours.

Life isn't fair! We have heard the line countless times. Perhaps we have voiced the words ourselves. And the words are true! Life is unjust. And a Christian faith worth its salt admits it. The great playwrights have tried their hand at solving the riddle, beginning with the author of the Book of Job and continuing through Archibald MacLeish's *JB.* To paraphrase some lines of the late Harry Emerson Fosdick, this is a world in which Socrates drinks the poison hemlock and Joan of Arc perishes in flames. We may add that it is a world in which one saintly friend, who never smoked cigarettes, died of cancer, and another, who never drank alcohol, had life snuffed out by a drunk driver.

The workers who picked grapes all day received a denarius. It was evidently the daily wage of a laborer in those

times—just enough to keep body and soul together and provide food and shelter for the family. They "filed their complaint" when those who had labored for just one hour not only
were paid first but also received the same amount.

Not fair? The employing householder reminds the unhappy laborers that their contract calls for a wage of one
denarius for a full day's work. He adds, "Am I not allowed to do
what I choose with what belongs to me? Or do you begrudge
my generosity?" (RSV).

The parable is not a model for labor negotiations, or a
guideline for labor-management relations, or a blueprint for
the economics of the modern business world. No, the point of
the parable has to do with life in the kingdom of God. God's
grace is for the undeserving as well as for those who think that
they have earned their place. Now, the twelve-hour workers
might well quote the advertisement, "We make money the
old-fashioned way. We earn it." But those who enter God's
realm are (with an eye to John 1:13) "born not of blood, or of
the will of the flesh, or of the will of man"—or of the work of
one's hands, or of the goodness of one's character, or of the
duration of one's service in God's vineyard—"but of God."

Matthew sets this parable in the midst of the disciples'
reactions to Jesus' comment after the rich man departs. Jesus
tells the disciples that a rich person (by his riches) cannot enter
the kingdom of heaven. One cannot buy his way or her way
into the divine realm any more easily than a camel can go
through the eye of a needle. What about us, the disciples ask?
Led by Peter, they want to know what their rewards, what their
wages will be in light of all their sacrifices. Jesus assures them
that their rewards will be great, culminating in the gift of
eternal life.

This parable, then, is for disciples—ancient and modern—and for the righteous, faithful, dutiful worker in all of us.
At the portal of the kingdom we have no rights, we possess no
merit, we produce no work, we earn no wages which guarantee
entrance. Before God anything we get paid is too much!
Suzanne de Dietrich writes, "And those who believe that they
enter it 'by right' strongly risk being among the last."[27] In the

THE SCANDAL OF GRACE

words of an old hymn, "Nothing in my hand I bring, Simply to Thy cross I cling."

What do we work for, when we work? Those laborers in the vineyard who are working under contract appear to be working for wages. Those who are forced by circumstance to wait until the final hour before being called to the vineyard appear to be working on faith and out of gratitude. The master tells the workers called at various times during the day: "Whatever is right I will give you." Motivation for service differs from person to person. Recall the three masons in a modern parable who are working on a building project. When asked what they are doing, the first says, "I am laying bricks." The second responds, "I am building this wall." The third answers, "I am building a temple."

What are we working *for?* There is a story of a missionary returning by ship to China. On board he meets a corporate executive whose company is seeking to expand its business in China. The businessman is impressed by the missionary's vast knowledge of Chinese culture, customs, history, and language. "Come to work for me and I will pay you five times what the church pays you." The missionary without hesitation declines. "What's wrong?" the man asks, "Is the salary I offer too small?" The missionary replies, "No, the salary is large enough. But the job is too small." God's realm is the same for all. The rewards are not payment for service rendered but gifts which we do not earn. Clearly, some work for gain, others for gold, and some out of gratitude.

What are we expecting for our labors? Those under contract in the vineyard expect a denarius . . . until, that is, they see those who have worked only a part of the day receive a full denarius. Then the full-day laborers expect more. In their disappointment they complain. Like them, we divide people into the more deserving and the less deserving. This happens at home, in school, and at work. We expect rewards and recognition to be proportionate. We want "the pie sliced" accordingly. We are not prepared for another kind of measuring stick. Two brothers were eating the lunch prepared for them by their mother before she left on an errand. For dessert she set out two pieces of pie, one larger than the other. The younger brother reached out quickly and took the larger piece. The older boy, irritated, issued this reprimand: "Don't you know that when there are two pieces you are supposed to take the smaller one?" The younger brother asked, "Which one would you have taken?" Big brother replied, "The smaller piece, of course." "Then why are you complaining? You have it!" End of argument! But not the end of hard feelings! Expectations die hard. But in the language of God's realm, another reward is given. Not a denarius, but grace!

Is there no salve to soothe the wounded spirit of a righteous Pharisee or a faithful disciple? As Luke tells it, a penitent thief from his cross—asking for a blessing in this final moment of his life, and receiving the promise of Paradise (a home fit for the righteous!)—enters Paradise. But is it possible that not as much Paradise enters him as enters the life-long disciple? The water is the same in a quart jar as in a gallon jug, yet the gallon jug has a greater capacity. Perhaps a Peter or James or John or Mary, because of the life-long working of God's Spirit in his or her life, will possess a greater capacity to experience eternal life—now and in heaven—than a penitent thief.

But we should not cover over the sting and jab of this story about laborers in a vineyard. In the realm of God our pay is always too much. Or, in the words of the apostle Paul: " . . . by grace you have been saved through faith, and this is not your own doing; it is the gift of God—not the result of works, so that no one may boast" (Eph 2:8–9 NRSV).

For Further Reading

Breech, *Silence of Jesus*, 142–57.

Donahue, *Gospel in Parable*, 79–85.

Eugene L. Lowry, in *How to Preach a Parable: Designs for Narrative Sermons* (ed. Eugene L. Lowry; Nashville: Abingdon, 1989) 115–31.

Perkins, *Hearing the Parables of Jesus*, 137–46.

Eduard Schweizer, *The Good News according to Matthew* (Atlanta: John Knox, 1975) 390–95.

Scott, *Hear Then the Parable*, 281–98.

Barbara Brown Taylor, in *A Chorus of Witnesses* (ed. Long and
Plantinga) 12–20.
Via, *The Parables*, 147–55.

ON BEING A PRODIGAL FATHER (LUKE 15:11–32)

Translation

*There once was a man who had two sons. And the younger of the
two said to his father, "Father, give me the share of the property
that falls to me." And so he divided his living between them. And a
few days later, when he had gathered everything, the younger son
went away into a distant country, and there he squandered*[28] *his
property by living dissolutely. And when he had spent it all, there
was a severe famine throughout that region, and he began to
experience want. So he went out and got himself hired by one of the
citizens of that region, who sent him into his fields to feed pigs. And
he longed to be fed from the carob pods that the pigs would eat, yet
no one gave him [anything].*[29]

*And when he had come to himself, he said, "How many of my
father's hired hands have more than enough food,*[30] *while I am
perishing here from hunger! I will get up and go to my father and
say to him, 'Father, I sinned against heaven and before you; I am no
longer worthy to be called your son. Make me as one of your hired
hands.'" And he got up and came to his own father. But while he
was still far away, his father saw him and was moved to pity,*[31] *and
running up he put his arms around his neck*[32] *and kissed him. And
the son said to him, "Father, I sinned against heaven and before
you; I am no longer worthy to be called your son." But the father
said to his servants, "Quick! Bring out the most important robe and
put it on him; and get the ring for his hand and sandals for his feet;
and bring the fatted calf, kill [it], and let's eat and celebrate! For
this, my son, was dead and came to life again; he was lost and has
been found." And they began to celebrate.*

*Now his older son was in the field, and when he came near the
house, he heard music and dancing. So calling over one of the
servants, he asked what this meant. And he told him, "Your brother
has come, and your father killed the fatted calf because he received
him back in good health." And he was angry and did not want to go
in, but his father came out and was pleading with him. But he*

answered his father, "Look, how many years do I serve you, and not once do I disobey your command—and not once did you give me a kid so that I could celebrate with my friends. But when this son of yours came—who devoured your living with prostitutes—for him you killed the fatted calf!" And he said to him, "Child, you are with me always, and everything that is mine is yours. But it was necessary to celebrate and rejoice, because this, your brother, was dead and came alive, lost and was found."

An Interpretation

This longest and best known of Jesus' parables generally carries the title "the prodigal son." The younger son, whose misadventures create the plot of the story, is indeed "prodigal," that is, wasteful. After all, he squanders his entire inheritance! Nevertheless, the truly prodigal figure, and also the central character, of the parable is the father of these two quite different sons.[33] It is the father whose excessive extravagance—of mercy—qualifies him as truly prodigal. And it is in this way that a familiar story becomes a genuinely difficult saying of Jesus.

When our approach to this parable is guided by Luke's reading of it—displayed in the composition of chapter 15 of his gospel—we hear the story as the final, climactic piece in a trilogy celebrating God's merciful acceptance of the "lost" in the ministry of Jesus. So the lost sheep (15:3–7), lost coin (15:8–10), and lost or prodigal son (15:11–32) all serve as metaphors for lost human beings, for those "sinners" (transgressors of the Torah) whom Jesus embraces in his ministry of healing, teaching, and meal fellowship. Together, the three parables defend Jesus' conduct—his association with sinners—against the barbs of scribes and Pharisees (15:1–2). The point, then, is that Jesus involves himself with the irreligious (and intimately at that—meal fellowship!) because God has forgiven them and reserved for them a place in the company of the saved (at the feast of the "reign of God").

As the culminating member in this trilogy, the parable of the prodigal son lends both poignancy and urgency to Jesus' message for his righteous critics. The intensely human drama that unfolds from the first line until the last cannot fail to engage the deepest emotions of the hearer. For the story concerns those relationships and values that lie at the heart of Jesus' culture (and our own): the integrity of the family, and of one's religious community; love and respect between father and son, brother and brother (we may extend the parable to embrace relationships among mothers, daughters, and sisters); and provision for the future well-being of the family. But the parable also advances beyond the first two in its final, urgent appeal to the older brother to be reconciled to his wayward younger brother. So the conclusion of chapter 15 returns full circle to its beginning: Jesus implores the righteous to accept the wayward to whom he has offered God's gracious acceptance. And like the parable of the vineyard workers, this story ends by leaving the final response of the offended righteous party in doubt. In this way the parable lays its appeal at the feet of the hearer. Now the hearer must decide whether to go in to the feast or remain outside, unreconciled to father and brother alike.

The parable already risks offending the listener. For who (except, perhaps, a restored prodigal) would not share the older brother's complaint at this unjust turning of the tables? Honor for the son who dishonored his family, and a public rebuke for the son who fulfilled his family and community obligations! But there is more here, and the issue of honor and shame is the key.

The prodigal son is a source of shame for himself and for his family. His list of "crimes" is long and egregious; long after his departure, his shameful conduct will be remembered in the town. First of all, by asking not only for a division in the estate which he and his older brother will inherit,[34] but also for the right to dispose of his share now, he has in effect treated his father as dead.[35] The older brother's later indictment of "this son of yours" has real force (whether or not the mention of prostitutes is accurate): he has "devoured *your living* with prostitutes" (15:30). The prodigal son has treated his father with utter contempt, to the point of disposing of his share of the estate while his father is still alive,[36] and so also jeopardizing the future security of the entire family. After leaving home, of course, the younger son goes from bad to worse, hitting bottom as a feeder of pigs for a gentile boss. He has deserted family, and now he forsakes his religious community and his faith as well. Hunger in time of famine is the least of his problems, though it does turn out to be the stimulus for change and a return home.

Yet the father, too, has brought shame to his name. His willingness to give the younger son his property early certainly proved to be foolish (cf. the warning in Sir 33:19–23!). But what brings disgrace to the father is his effusive behavior at the return of his wayward son. The images are graphic: running out to meet the prodigal; an affectionate public embrace; restoration to the position of honored son (using the tokens of the best robe, the ring, and the sandals); and a festive dinner party celebrating the return of one who had (after "killing" his father)[37] been as good as dead. No wonder that the older son should object. It is not good for morale! The obedient, responsible son feels taken for granted, while this spectacular sinner who has made the family a laughing-stock basks in the glory. Without question, the father has been excessive in mercy, in generosity to one who had shamed and manipulated him. It is the father who is truly prodigal.

And that is the point. God's treatment of the disobedient, of wayward "sinners"—at least in Jesus' vision of God's reign *and in his practice of it*—cannot fail to offend the righteous. Pharisee and tax collector, full-day vineyard worker and one-hour worker, older and younger son: again and again is enacted the dynamic of reversal. The undeserving receive surprising grace, and so the deserving are scandalized. It is not an approach likely to ensure popularity among those who, like Jesus, take their religion seriously. But it is Jesus' way. God is prodigal in grace toward sinful human beings. The challenge is to see oneself—no matter how impeccable one's life or religion—in the ranks of the undeserving. Having felt outrage at the scandal of grace, one is then moved to celebrate God's merciful acceptance of all who respond to divine love, *including oneself.*

From Text to Sermon: "Lost and Found"

Things have a way of getting lost. In a recent "Lost and Found" column in the Classified Ads of a daily newspaper, the "Lost" included five cats, twenty-one dogs, one bird, a billfold, and a bracelet. The "Found" listed four cats, eighteen dogs, and a passport. People often leave items in church buildings. Some time ago the sexton of one church found a large package of "green stamps" in a pew after morning worship. He brought them to the pastor and exclaimed, "What do people think this is—a redemption center?"

People, too, have a way of getting lost. Chapter 15 of Luke's gospel is the "Lost and Found" Department of the Bible. Here Jesus tells stories about a lost sheep, a lost coin, and a lost son.

The sheep is one out of a flock of one hundred. It is a symbol of the person who gets lost *in the crowd*.[38] Only one in a hundred! Or a thousand. Or 250 million. Just a drop in the bucket. The size of an atom. A person who feels that she or he does not count. Schools and corporations and churches are full of people lost in the crowd.

The silver coin is one out of ten owned by a poor woman. One day it slips through her fingers and rolls across the hard earthen floor and disappears. The coin is a symbol of the person who becomes lost *by the crowd*. Through no fault of the individual, he or she is overlooked, bypassed, snubbed. Children may be lost in the shambles of a broken home or by neglect or by over-indulgence. A mother said to a judge before whom her delinquent son stood, "I don't know why he gets into trouble. We've always given him everything he ever wanted." Tragically, some people are lost by the church. In a typical church, half the persons who come into membership through the front door go out the back door, becoming inactive members.

We call the lost son "prodigal." Apparently he finds life too dull and drab on the farm. The days are filled with drudgery. So he asks for his share of the family estate in cash, and then goes into a far country. There he spends all his money in "dissolute living." His fair-weather friends disappear, leaving him lonely and alone. This young man is a symbol of the person lost *with the crowd*. Peer pressure and crowd mentality prevail. How often parents hear the lines, "Everybody is doing it. Everyone is going." "Somebody" does the thinking, trend setting, and fad fashioning for everyone else. Not just young people feel this pressure; adults, too, go along with the crowd. We take our cues from commercials. We become chameleons of creature culture. Each may choose his or her own "far country." Each may choose or drift into a particular path the crowd takes. Like the prodigal son, a person becomes lost with the crowd.

Can the lost be found? Is the sheep really lost if it remembers the sound of the shepherd's voice, and if that shepherd is out in the hills and wilderness looking for it and calling it by name? Is a person lost in the crowd actually lost if someone (or Someone) believes that the person does count—does have worth, is a child of the Creator? God pays attention to little things—lilies and leaves and blades of grass. God's eye is on the sparrow. God is the Good Shepherd, who rejoices when one out of one hundred is found.

Is the coin really lost if it is stamped with the image and inscription of the king, and if the woman is searching every nook and corner until she finds it? Is the individual lost by the crowd really lost if she or he bears the image of God, marred though it may be? Is the person really lost if there are people who say, "We are sorry that we hurt you and let you down?" If someone cares or speaks or shares or invites or welcomes? If someone forgives and loves and embraces? The Maker of all things takes the fragile and fractured life and makes "all things new." Joy in heaven breaks out because a person begins again.

Is the young man lost with the crowd in a far country and in a herd of swine really lost if he remembers his name and his roots and knows where home is? If he has a father or mother waiting and watching and praying for the son to come "to himself" and come home? Is the person lost with the crowd really lost if our heavenly Father has a light in the window and waits with amazing grace and open arms? If someone or some group in the community has a word other than condemnation?

If the neighbors give the person a chance? If church members look with something other than a cold stare, or speak kind words rather than repeat vicious gossip? If parents and acquaintances and church people forgive?

But the stories in Luke's fifteenth chapter are not ended. Jesus tells the story of the prodigal's older brother. He is the family's "pride and joy." He stays on the farm. He works hard. He is obedient. He is upright in character. He never gets into trouble. When his brother returns, he comes back from a long day in the fields, only to hear the sound of music and laughter. A servant explains, "Your brother has come." Your father is welcoming him with a big party—beef barbecue, a top band, new clothes, a gold ring, a dance for the whole neighborhood.

The older brother is incensed. His father's attempts to appease him have no effect; he refuses to go in to honor one whom he no longer regards as his brother ("This son of yours . . . "). He wants no part of this welcome home to the "black sheep" of the family who has wasted his life—his father's life!—on "wine, women, and song." So he separates himself from the scandalous affair going on in his own home.

The older brother is a symbol of the person lost *from the crowd*. This is one who thinks he or she is different and better and more holy. This self-appraisal may be true, indeed (even as it was for the Pharisee at prayer in the temple): sterling character, spotless reputation, excellent work habits, high ideals, exemplary conduct.

And this brings us to the reason Jesus told these stories. Luke informs us that the so-called outcasts and outsiders were flocking to Jesus. "And the Pharisees and the scribes were grumbling and saying, 'This fellow welcomes sinners and eats with them.' " Jesus' response? These three parables (Luke 15). Perhaps Jesus' hearers were disturbed most when, in the parable of the prodigal son, the father says, "This, my son, was dead and came to life again; he was lost and has been found." The celebration and the merriment seemed out of place. Why not a party for the son who stayed home, worked diligently, and kept out of trouble? Why the fuss over the boy who turned his father's hair grey and aged his mother beyond her years and squandered the family fortune?

Can we live with the offense of grace? Jesus said, "I tell you, there will be more joy in heaven over one sinner who repents than over ninety-nine righteous persons who need no repentance." What are we to do with such a God?

Some years ago, a boy and a girl came to see me in my study. He was seventeen; she was sixteen. They wanted to be married. The girl said, "I know we're young, but we're in love and I am pregnant." I explained that they had other options, that they did not "have to get married." Her mother, who had been waiting outside the office, joined us, and as we all talked, I became convinced that, young as they were, these two possessed a quality of love and an understanding of commitment beyond their years. I agreed to marry them after they had come for several counseling sessions. In one of those sessions the girl said, "My mother tells me that I cannot be married in the chapel because I am pregnant." I said, "Of course, you can be married in the chapel. That is why the church has this chapel: so that you may be married in it." Later in the same session, she said, "My mother tells me that because I am pregnant I cannot be married in a white dress." I replied, "Of course you may be married in a white dress. That is why Jesus came to earth and died on the cross: so that you might be married in a white dress." I think the Holy Spirit rather than my own dull mind prompted me to quote the lines from Isaiah: "Though your sins are like scarlet, they shall be as white as snow; though they are red like crimson, they shall become like wool" (Isa 1:18 RSV). Tears flowed down her cheeks. I knew in that moment that if this sixteen-year-old girl never again understood the wonder of God's love, she knew it in that instant.

When God's grace offends one person, it well may bring joy and life to another. Pharisees and theologians and "good church folk" should not want to be "the older brother." We—all of us—can and must live with the offense of grace . . . if we are to live at all. Only so will we experience the joy heaven knows at the coming home of all God's children. Home to our prodigal father.

For Further Reading

Kenneth E. Bailey, *Poet and Peasant* (Grand Rapids: Eerdmans, 1976) 158–206.

Breech, *Silence of Jesus*, 184–214.

Donahue, *Gospel in Parable*, 151–62.

Fitzmyer, *Gospel according to Luke*, 2.1082–94.

Jeremias, *Rediscovering the Parables*, 101–105.

Schweizer, *Good News according to Luke*, 246–52.

Scott, *Hear Then the Parable*, 99–125.

Mary Ann Tolbert, *Perspectives on the Parables: An Approach to Multiple Interpretations* (Philadelphia: Fortress, 1979) 93–114.

ENDNOTES

[1] So, for example, Joseph A. Fitzmyer, *The Gospel according to Luke: Introduction, Translation, and Notes* (AB 28–28A; 2 vols; Garden City, N.Y.: Doubleday, 1981–85) 2.884–85; and I. Howard Marshall, *Commentary on Luke* (NIGTC 3; Grand Rapids: Eerdmans, 1978) 444–45.

[2] Indeed, such a reading of the parable, in the light of its narrative context in Luke, informs the homiletical reflections offered below ("From Text to Sermon"). This understanding of the Samaritan as model of compassion has been a significant factor in altruistic behavior in American society (see Robert Wuthnow, *Acts of Compassion: Caring for Others and Helping Ourselves* [Princeton: Princeton University, 1991] 157–87). Note, however, Joel B. Green's cautionary remarks on this interpretation of the parable in its context in Luke's gospel (*The Theology of the Gospel of Luke* [NTT; Cambridge: Cambridge University, 1995] 129–30, 139).

[3] So also Scott, *Hear Then the Parable*, 194.

[4] This is a generous reading of the priestly functionaries' actions. Lev 21:1–2 stipulates that a priest may not "defile himself for a dead person among his relatives," except for immediate family. The high priest is to avoid contact with the dead body of even a father or mother (Lev 21:11). Nevertheless, in view of the special importance given to burial in Jewish culture, it is not clear that they thus escape blame. Note, for example, m. *Berakot* 3.1: "One whose dead is lying before him [awaiting burial] is exempt from 1. the recitation of the Shema, 2. and from [wearing] phylacteries" (translation from Jacob Neusner,

The Mishnah [New Haven: Yale University Press, 1988] 6). And according to later Jewish interpretations of this text in Leviticus, there are exceptions to the command that a priest not "defile himself for the dead among his people." The tractate *Nazir* in the Mishnah (compiled about 200 CE, but containing earlier traditions) records a debate over the question whether even a high priest should contract uncleanness by handling a neglected corpse, with R. Eliezer arguing that he should (*Nazir* 7.1; see Neusner, *The Mishnah*, 443). If the priest and the Levite believe the man is dead, it may be that they have an obligation to see to the corpse's burial. See further Scott, *Hear Then the Parable*, 195–97.

⁵ The pattern "priest, Levite, Israelite" is conventional. See the discussion in Scott, *Hear Then the Parable*, 198.

⁶ Not that love of enemy is an easy achievement. Indeed, perhaps it is the experience—in parable—of compassion at the hands of one I am inclined to despise that creates for me even the possibility of love of the enemy.

⁷ Of course, the roots of this mutual antagonism lie in the rivalry of northern and southern kingdoms earlier in Israel's history, and hostilities were sharpened by the existence of rival centers of worship in Jerusalem and Shechem. In 128 BCE the Hasmonean ruler of Judea, John Hyrcanus, destroyed the Samaritans' temple at Shechem, an event which further damaged Jewish-Samaritan relations. Although the Samaritans revered the Pentateuch (the first five books of Jewish Scripture, or Torah), Jewish people perceived their temple worship as illegitimate (this assumption underlies the conversation narrated in John 4:20–22) and the people themselves not as true Jews but as foreigners. For a brief sketch of Samaritan origins and history, see James D. Purvis, "Samaritans," *HBD*, 898–900. See also Helmut Koester, *Introduction to the New Testament* (Philadelphia: Fortress, 1982), vol. 1, *History, Culture, and Religion of the Hellenistic Age*, 247–49.

⁸ Translation by Jacob Neusner, *The Mishnah*, 87.

⁹ Edwin Markham, "Outwitted," printed in *The Best Loved Poems of the American People* (ed. Hazel Felleman; Garden City, N.Y.: Doubleday, 1936).

¹⁰ The expression "the Pharisee, standing by himself" (v. 11) is parallel to "the tax collector, standing far off" (v. 13). This parallelism indicates that the phrase *pros heauton* ("by [to] himself") in v. 11 describes the Pharisee's location, rather than presenting him as the party addressed by the prayer. Several modern translations (e.g., the RSV, Phillips, and Fitzmyer's Anchor Bible translation [*Gospel according to Luke*, 2.1186]) have the Pharisee praying to, with, or about himself.

¹¹ This saying appears also in Luke 14:11 (and cf. Matt 23:12).

¹² In numerous publications (e.g., *Paul and Palestinian Judaism* [Philadelphia: Fortress, 1977] and *Jesus and Judaism* [Philadelphia: Fortress, 1983]), E. P. Sanders has insisted forcefully on the necessity of

reconceptualizing Pharisaic Judaism (and other forms of early Judaism as well). For a brief introduction to Sanders's work, see his article "Judaism and the Grand 'Christian' Abstractions: Love, Mercy, and Grace," in *Int* 39 (1985) 357–72. Also useful is Anthony J. Saldarini's discussion of "Pharisees" in *HBD*, 782–83.

[13] A strikingly similar prayer of thanksgiving appears in the Babylonian Talmud, tractate *Berakot* 28b, where a rabbi thanks God for the blessing that comes to him because his life has been devoted to the study of the Torah, while others follow a life of frivolity to destruction.

[14] The Torah called for an annual fast on the Day of Atonement (see Lev 16:29,31; 23:27,29,32; Num 29:7). See also the helpful notes by Fitzmyer (*Gospel according to Luke*, 2.1187).

[15] In the Babylonian Talmud, tractate *Sanhedrin* (25b), tax collectors are among those said to be disqualified from service as witnesses or judges because of their occupation as "robbers." For a brief but helpful sketch of the system of taxation in Roman Palestine at the time of Jesus, and of popular Jewish attitudes toward tax collectors, see John E. Stambaugh and David L. Balch, *The New Testament in Its Social Environment* (LEC 2; Philadelphia: Westminster, 1986) 77–78; Saldarini, "Publicans," *HBD*, 841.

[16] That is, at about 9:00 a.m.

[17] The narration shifts to the present tense for the verbs in vv. 6b–8. Such usage of the historical present lends immediacy and vividness to the story, and in this case it also casts the spotlight on the pivotal interchange between the householder and his one-hour "day" laborers (vv. 6–7), and on the suspenseful summons to the workers to claim their wages (v. 8).

[18] This explicit directive to pay the last hired first may strike some readers as odd, even objectionable. Has the owner deliberately sought to provoke these laborers who, in their own words, "have borne the burden of the day and the scorching heat" (v. 12), by stirring within them expectations of generous pay beyond the terms originally agreed? Or is Matthew himself responsible for the order of payment? Thus he sets the stage for the saying with which he clinches the parable (v. 16): "So the last will be first and the first will be last." We believe the order of payment is a necessary part of the story's plot. The last–first inversion creates suspense: Will the owner be just as generous with the workers hired earlier, going beyond the original terms? In fact, if payment were received in the order of hire, there would be no parable! (cf. Perkins, *Hearing the Parables of Jesus*, 139; Schweizer, *Good News according to Matthew*, 392; Scott, *Hear Then the Parable*, 294; Dan O. Via, *The Parables: Their Literary and Existential Dimension* [Philadelphia: Fortress, 1967] 148–49). The point of the story concerns the apparent injustice done to the twelve-hour laborers, *as they see it*. But

they must first know of the vineyard owner's relative generosity to the one-hour workers before they have any reason to protest.

[19] Crossan (*In Parables: The Challenge of the Historical Jesus* [New York: Harper & Row, 1973] 111–13) and Scott (*Hear Then the Parable,* 285–87), among others, have argued, on the basis of the language used (e.g., the antithesis "good" vs. "evil"), that Matt 20:14–15 is secondary, added by Matthew to the original story. Matthew has retold the parable, to be sure, and does add v. 16 to emphasize the theme of role inversion (cf. Matt 19:30); nevertheless, comparison with the closing dialogue between father and older son in Luke 15:29–32 suggests that vv. 14–15 may belong to the original structure of the parable (see Perkins, *Hearing the Parables of Jesus,* 137–38). In each parable ending, the character accused of unjust action (the householder in Matt 20:1–15, the father in Luke 15:11–32) explains/defends his benevolent treatment of the needy party (the one-hour workers; the younger son). And with the explanation comes an implicit appeal for a changed heart in the dutiful (the all-day laborers; the older son).

[20] We must assume that the promise received by workers hired at the third hour, "I will pay you whatever is right," extends also to those hired later in the day (see v. 5). It is striking that the workers hired last are simply told to go into the vineyard; there is not a word about payment (an omission corrected by some later manuscripts). This silence certainly heightens the suspense about the treatment they will receive. Because after this point the parable throws the spotlight on those hired at dawn and those hired near evening, leaving the intermediate groups out of view, the contrast is especially stark. The heart of the parable, therefore, is its resolution of this tensive contrast between early morning workers, who *know* what they will receive, and part-day workers, who must rely on the benevolence of the vineyard owner.

[21] Jeremias (*Rediscovering the Parables,* 28) conjectures that the owner awarded a full day's pay to all the laborers out of pity for their poverty, but the parable does not say as much. Indeed, it does not probe the motivation behind this unusual action; all weight falls on the initiative and freedom of the vineyard owner, whatever his motives. Not even the apparent urgency of these hirings—to the point of finding additional laborers for an hour's work—is explained to the hearer. Is this actually the time of harvest, and the onset of the rainy season calls for urgent action (suggested, e.g., by Jeremias, *Rediscovering the Parables,* 108–9)? But then why have so many workers been standing idle in the marketplace throughout the day? About many such questions the parable—like other good stories—remains silent, teasing the hearer to apply his or her own creative imagination in making sense of the narrated events.

[22] Scholars who have read the story in this way include John P. Meier (*Matthew* [NTM 3; Wilmington, Del.: Michael Glazier, 1980]

224–26) and Eta Linnemann (*Jesus of the Parables* [New York: Harper & Row, 1966] 84), among many others. Scott's critique of this interpretation is helpful but, in our view, too sharply drawn (see *Hear Then the Parable*, 282–84). Jeremias emphasizes the generosity of the householder, even naming this parable the "parable of the good employer" (*Rediscovering the Parables*, 108), yet he is also well aware that the "good employer" displays measured, not unlimited generosity (p. 28). Jeremias observes that a subsistence wage, and nothing more, is paid; nevertheless, it remains significant that a subsistence wage is paid even to one-hour laborers who, in the prevailing economic system, could scarcely lay rightful claim to it. If not in the case of the full-day workers, certainly in the case of the one-hour workers the householder's action must be described as relatively generous. Still, the chief issue here is not the householder's generosity in itself, but the contrasting treatments given these two groups.

[23] Via (*The Parables*, 147–55) reads the parable in this way. This interpretation places too much weight on the final command, "Take what is yours and go." Even if the parable originally ended here (at v. 14a: so Scott, *Hear Then the Parable*, 282), there is no indication that the dismissal involves a permanent exclusion. And if the subsequent remarks by the landowner—explaining or justifying his action (vv. 14b–15)—belong to the original form of the parable, then, as in the case of the parable of the "prodigal son," we are left with a figure accused of injustice appealing for *metanoia*, a transformed perception, on the part of a slighted party. In other words, the story has an open ending, with the final response of the angry workers (Luke 15: older brother) remaining unknown. Via is correct to insist (see also Schweizer, *Good News according to Matthew*, 390–95) that the vineyard workers are offended by the owner's show of grace to the less deserving. We believe, however, that the path to reconciliation is left open; the hearer must decide the issue.

[24] This is so whether we believe or whether we doubt the one-hour workers' excuse for their day's idleness ("nobody hired us"). The contrast between them and the full-day laborers shows that they have not earned the denarius given them by the householder.

[25] Or divine judgment! On the vineyard as metaphor for Israel, see, e.g., Isa 5:1–7; Jer 2:20–21; 5:10; 12:10; Hos 10:1.

[26] Many scholars find the original setting of the parable of the vineyard workers in Jesus' defense of his association with sinners. See, e.g., Jeremias, *Rediscovering the Parables*, 29, 108; John C. Fenton, *Saint Matthew* (PNTC; New York: Penguin, 1963) 319; Schweizer, *Good News according to Matthew*, 394; Via, *The Parables*, 149–50.

[27] *Matthew* (LBC 16; Richmond: John Knox, 1961) 105.

[28] Literally, "he scattered," the same verb used of the steward accused before the rich man in Luke 16:1–8a.

[29] All the verbs in this sentence appear in the imperfect tense; that is, they point to repeated action, to an ongoing situation of need, unsatisfied desire, and failure to respond.

[30] Literally, "bread (loaves)."

[31] This is the same verb used of the "good Samaritan" in Luke 10:33.

[32] Literally, "he fell upon his neck."

[33] Jeremias terms this the "parable of the Father's Love" (*Rediscovering the Parables*, 101).

[34] Since the family in this parable has only two sons, the younger son will receive one-third of the inheritance, his older brother two-thirds. See Fitzmyer, *Gospel according to Luke*, 2.1087. For helpful discussion of the traditional theme of the younger and older brothers, see Scott, *Hear Then the Parable*, 111–13.

[35] See Jeremias, *Rediscovering the Parables*, 101; Scott, *Hear Then the Parable*, 109–11; Bailey, *Poet and Peasant*, 164–65; but cf. Fitzmyer, *Gospel according to Luke*, 2.1087.

[36] It appears that even in a case such as this, where the father gives property to an heir before his death, the father retains the right to maintain himself from the property; the interest from the property is legally his. See Fitzmyer, *Gospel according to Luke*, 2.1087; Scott, *Hear Then the Parable*, 109–11. The younger son's actions in this story ignore such concerns altogether.

[37] See Scott, *Hear Then the Parable*, 111.

[38] I am indebted for some of the symbolism in these sermon reflections to a message I heard years ago by the late Ralph W. Sockman, long-time Methodist minister of Christ Church in New York City.

THE COST OF GRACE:
DEMANDS OF DISCIPLESHIP

*Whoever comes to me and does not hate his
own father and mother, wife and children,
brothers and sisters, yes, and even life itself,
cannot be my disciple. (Luke 14:26)*

T HE PARABLES OF JESUS WITH WHICH WE HAVE WRESTLED IN THE
previous chapter were "hard" because they seemed too
"easy"—too easy, that is, on those who have not taken seriously
their community responsibilities, their religion, their God. Jesus'
word surprised, stunned, and even angered the righteous with
its offer of forgiveness for sinners and new life in the company
of God's people. Jesus enacted this scandalizing word of grace
in his public ministry, with cures for the sick, assurance for
scorned outsiders, and meals shared with the "wrong" people.
Modern readers confronted with such a radical message of
grace may protest that this is "cheap grace" (to use Dietrich
Bonhoeffer's apt phrase). Or to borrow a rhetorical question
from Paul, "Why not go on sinning, then, so that grace may
increase?" (Rom 6:1).

The sayings of Jesus to be explored in this chapter put to
rest any impression that Jesus, with his free offer of mercy for
the undeserving, simply winks at human sin. Consider, for
example, the stern warning: "Not everyone who says to me,
'Lord, Lord,' will enter the kingdom of heaven, but only the
one who does the will of my Father in heaven" (Matt 7:21).
Jesus reinforces that warning (in Matthew's arrangement of the

sayings [7:24–27; cf. Luke 6:47–49]) with a parable about two home builders, one of whom constructs his house on sand, while the other gives his house a foundation of rock. Naturally, fierce wind and flood demolish the house built on sand, but the house erected on a solid foundation still remains standing when nature's fury has been spent. With this graphic image Jesus warns those who come to him, hear his message, but then fail to live according to that message. It matters what we do!

The surprising grace of God comes to one who does not deserve it, but then God claims one's life—claims one's entire life, as we soon will see. In fact, it turns out that the grace of which Jesus speaks and which he enacts in his ministry exacts from those who would listen and follow a great cost. Many of Jesus' difficult sayings are difficult precisely because they are so challenging, so demanding, so impossibly demanding. The demands of discipleship are weighty, indeed: "strenuous commands," as Anthony Harvey puts it in the title of his helpful study.[1] Our concern in this chapter, then, is the "cost of grace"—the demanding discipleship to which Jesus summons those who would follow him.

FOR THE LOVE OF FAMILY (LUKE 14:26; MATT 10:37)

Translation

> If one comes to me and does not hate his own father and mother and wife and children and brothers and sisters—and even his own life—he cannot be my disciple. (Luke 14:26)

> One who loves father or mother more than me is not worthy of me, and one who loves son or daughter more than me is not worthy of me. (Matt 10:37)

An Interpretation

We may as well get right to the heart of things. In this saying, recorded somewhat differently by Luke and Matthew, Jesus seems to advocate—indeed, to insist on—hatred of one's own parents. This is, of course, shocking in itself, and runs counter to the received wisdom of every human culture I know or can imagine. But there is more. Jesus appears to be setting himself against Scripture, against God's command. After all, the command to honor parents was a central piece of the law of Moses (Exod 20:12; Deut 5:16).[2] Moreover, Jesus even seems to be contradicting himself. Elsewhere he is reported to have held up the command to honor parents as an example of the life of obedience which is necessary if one is to inherit eternal life (Mark 10:19; par. in Matt 19:19 and Luke 18:20). Are we to honor or hate our parents? What is more, are we to heed the word of one who would direct us to love enemies, yet hate our own fathers and mothers?

The problem is clear enough. Before we can fully grasp the meaning and force of this hard saying of Jesus, we will need to bring into view the sayings from Luke 9:59–62. Nevertheless, some preliminary comments on Luke 14:26 and Matt 10:37 may prove useful. It is obvious that these two texts form two versions of the same basic saying, in which Jesus placed relation to himself above relation to one's parents. Luke's form of the saying expands the range of family ties to include wife and siblings, while Matthew's version focuses on two sets of rela-tionships, each spanning a generation: parents and children, and those children with their own children.[3] There is another striking difference between the two texts: in Matthew Jesus warns against loving parents "more than me," whereas in Luke Jesus summons those who would follow him to "hate" parents.[4] This is an important clue to the meaning of the saying. What does Jesus *mean* when he speaks of hating father and mother?[5]

Matthew's form of the saying suggests that "to hate" is equivalent to "to love less." In another passage, Luke reflects the same usage: "No slave can serve two masters, for either he will hate one and love the other, or be devoted to one and despise the other; you cannot serve God and mammon" (Luke 16:13). There are two choices: love and hate. And the terms are both relational and relative. To love one person less than another is to "hate" him or her. In other words, I might love a person quite genuinely and yet, in view of another, higher loyalty, actually be said to hate the first individual. Therefore,

if Matthew's paraphrase captures the original force of Jesus'
saying, he was advocating not hatred of parents (in *any* sense the
word has for us today) but *a greater love for himself,* a higher
claim, a deeper loyalty, an overriding commitment of self to
his cause.

This discussion helps to bring Jesus' hard saying closer to
our sense of common decency, yet it does not remove all
difficulties. For Jesus here is calling into question crucially
important and fundamental values of his own culture, and of
our cultures today. We would do well to reflect more closely on
his message, and to do so it will be helpful to turn now to two
statements Jesus addressed to potential disciples,[6] according to
Luke 9:59–62 (our translation).

> [Jesus] said to another, "Follow me!" And he said, "Allow me first
> to go and bury my father." But [Jesus] said to him, "Leave the
> dead to bury their own dead, but you, you go and proclaim the
> reign of God!"
>
> And yet another said, "I will follow you, Lord [or 'Sir'], but
> first allow me to say good-bye to those in my home." Jesus said,
> though, "No one who puts his hand to the plow and looks back
> is fit for the realm of God."

These sayings are of one piece with the call to "hate"
father and mother. In each case, one's basic loyalty and devotion to family is jeopardized because Jesus claims that another
allegiance, another cause (his), transcends it. Once again, we
need to appreciate how demanding Jesus is here. Jesus sets his
word and his mission over against sacred, God-given duties
which are of cardinal importance to Jewish people of his day.
Burial of the dead was a religious duty above all other duties,
even study of the Torah.[7] Even priests, ordinarily forbidden to
touch a corpse, were permitted this contact in order to see to
the burial of a dead relative (with exemptions granted only to
the high priest and those fulfilling Nazirite vows).[8] So when a
potential disciple seeks to delay his journey with Jesus so that
he may bury his father, he is simply upholding fundamental
values of his culture, out of obedience to God and honor to his
parents. How could anyone challenge such time-honored values? And yet that is just what Jesus does![9]

The other encounter, in which Jesus refuses to permit a would-be follower to say good-bye to his family (Luke 9:61–62), is, at first glance, somewhat less troubling than the saying on burial of parents, for the social responsibility it subverts appears more commonplace and less "sacred." Nevertheless, this passage brings out with real force the separation from family that Jesus demands of disciples,[10] and that is no less troubling for us—or for Jesus' first hearers. It appears that we are challenged not only to surrender duties and obligations, but also to abandon our own families (much as in the hard saying about "hating" father and mother, son and daughter)! In the culture Jesus knew, the family was the center of one's life (remember, that is why the conduct of the "prodigal son" was so reprehensible).[11] Here again, Jesus relativizes something that had once seemed to be of supreme value. His call to "follow me" is even more important.

We have, then, a set of challenging sayings, in which Jesus forcefully places himself and the reality of God's rule above the very best of all human commitments and priorities.[12] And that is the point. In the world Jesus is creating for those who follow him, God's claim is above all other claims. God's rule demands one's ultimate commitment, and if this commitment clashes with any other (no matter how important), then that other allegiance must give way. But why does Jesus have to put it so sharply? Why such an extreme demand?[13] Why indeed. Jesus' call to discipleship is a summons to change, a call to experience the world in a new way, an invitation to a new understanding of God, an appeal to reorder human relationships in the light of this picture of God. Old patterns of life are tenacious, however, and old understandings of God do not die without a struggle. Jesus dares to replace our vision of things with a new one. Yet we cling stubbornly to our old way of seeing and discerning and valuing. And so Jesus, in challenging our familiar and comfortable world, can only succeed by making exaggerated claims, by painting extreme images. He must, in a word, *attack* the world that we have allowed to define us, the life we love so much, in order to give us a new life. He must pry us loose from the safe haven of our past if we are to be open to experience the reign of God.

Jesus' hard words like this are always to be taken seriously, but that does not necessarily mean taking them literally. Nor do these words become a new set of rules, a new code of laws governing family life in the kingdom of God. (If they were, would there be *any* family life in the realm of God?) No, the creative work of appropriating these hard sayings, of understanding the nature of Jesus' call to discipleship and responding within the circumstances of our own lives, must be left to each one of us. Does the call to follow Jesus always uproot from family? Certainly, for those who first heard this call, it *did* disrupt families and sometimes even sever family ties.[14] Yet many (no doubt most) modern readers will experience the summons to honor God above all else—to love God with the whole of one's being and with complete commitment—as a call back into the family rather than as a detachment from it. Indeed, one might *dishonor* God by using texts like these as a pretext for evading responsibilities to love, to nurture, to care within the family. That is to say, Jesus' hard sayings on parents and family challenge us to examine and reorder our commitments, our most important relationships, in view of the supreme claim of God upon our lives. They do not, however, legislate our response to that claim. Yet the clarion call does remain, and these hard sayings of Jesus remind us that no barrier to our commitment to the work of God's rule may be allowed to stand. That is the essence of discipleship. Following Jesus has its cost! In our study of Mark 9:42–48 (pp. 57–65), we will see that Jesus also uses exaggerated imagery to make the point that everything is at stake in our *participation in* the life of the kingdom. But before turning to that passage, we need to balance Jesus' "attack" upon the family with other sayings which uphold the crucial value and integrity of the family. These sayings on marriage and divorce, however, create their own problems! We tackle them in the next section.

From Text to Sermon: "The Cost of Grace and the Family: Encounters with Hyperbole"

Does Jesus want us to love our parents, spouse, and children? Right! Does he ask us to hate them? Right!

I am reminded of the father who brought a business acquaintance home for dinner. As they conversed in the den before the meal, the two brothers in the family became embroiled in a fierce argument. They ran to their father, each seeking his support. He turned to the younger son to hear his side of the argument, and then said, "Son, you're right." He turned to the older boy and, after listening to his side of the disagreement, said, "Son, you're right." The visitor, who had heard everything, addressed the father: "Look, they can't both be right." The father responded, "You're right!"

Jesus was on the way to the cross. That is, he had turned his face steadfastly toward Jerusalem. "Now large crowds were traveling with him" (Luke 14:25). Enthusiasm and excitement ran high. Not even his closest disciples comprehended what was ahead: a lonely figure on a cross between two thieves. The grace he had to give would cost his life at Calvary. The terrible cup of human sin which he would drink and the dark abyss of God-forsakenness which he would enter were beyond the understanding of fair-weather followers. How could the seed of the kingdom, falling on hardened hearts and shallow minds and cluttered lives, bear fruit? They were saying, as it were, "Lord, we will follow you, provided life can go on as usual and things can stay as they are."

According to Luke, Jesus responded with the shock treatment of hyperbole. "Whoever comes to me and does not hate his own father and mother, wife and children, brothers and sisters, yes, even life itself, cannot be my disciple."

The Lord got their attention, and he gets ours as well. First, we note, we dare not take his words literally, any more than we can take literally the claim of Jesus in John's gospel, "I am the gate" (John 10:9). Jesus, I believe, hated no one. He expects us to love our families and our neighbors *and* our enemies. He brought joy at a wedding. He sanctified the marriage relationship. According to John, he reached down in love to his mother from the cross (John 19:26–27). Even a financial vow to God, he declared, should not take precedence over support for one's mother or father (Mark 7:9–13).

No, the word about hate is not to be taken literally. Jesus uses the hyperbole of his Semitic culture. (The example of hyperbole given in Webster's New Collegiate Dictionary is fascinating: "mile-high ice cream cones."[15]) This is the point: love for Christ automatically classifies all other loves as lesser loves. Loyalty to Christ supersedes all other loyalties. Commitment to Christ categorizes all other commitments as secondary.

Second, we can understand what the cost of grace means by looking at the sacrifices men and women have made and continue to make in the pursuit of excellence. Albert Schweitzer loved music, philosophy, literature, and theology. He could have achieved fame and fortune in any one of these pursuits. But they became lesser loves in his choice of medicine and his desire to serve indigenous people in a remote part of Africa. His friends told him that he was throwing his life away. Indeed, this is what Schweitzer did. He lost his life and found it. All the other careers he might have chosen he "hated" in comparison with his healing ministry in the hospital at Lambarene.

Look at the autobiographies of recent or present great athletes: Gale Sayers and Earl Campbell in football; Orel Hershiser in baseball; Nancy Lopez in golf. And read the autobiography of Tom Landry, long-time coach of the Dallas Cowboys in the National Football League, who earlier had starred on the Longhorn football team at the University of Texas.[16] Each of these well-known persons, in his or her love of the sport, laid aside other options and can be characterized by such phrases as: total commitment, striving for perfection, complete dedication. Each loved or loves the same activities and interests which you and I may choose. But the one all-consuming priority made these activities and interests lesser loves.

We find the same love-hate pattern in any field to which we turn: science with an Albert Einstein; music with a Jascha Heifetz; art with a Raphael or a Georgia O'Keefe. Those of us who studied at the seminary in Princeton in the 1930s, 1940s, or early 1950s will never forget the great scientist Einstein's walks past the seminary. His dress consisted of a turtle-neck sweater, grey baggy pants, and plain slippers. His long grey hair surrendered to the direction in which the wind blew. He acknowledged greetings with a humble nod or word. Though his beloved violin helped him enjoy moments of relaxation, he lived his days in a world of mysterious hand-written mathematical symbols and figures, bent on finding the unifying principle of matter and energy, speed, and space. The world will never be the same, because his devotion to that search made all else a lesser love.

Third, we must face the implications of the cost of grace as we live our daily lives. Jesus Christ comes first! He learned in early childhood: "You shall love the Lord your God with all your heart, and with all your soul, and with all your might" (Deut 6:5). Later, in his public teaching, he would call this the "first commandment" and, according to Mark, expand it to include loving God "with all your mind" (Mark 12:30). We dare not pass over lightly the word "all." How easy it would be if the call to follow Jesus meant following him part of the time or being loyal most of the time or being true to him with half a mind or with half-hearted devotion.

Of course, Jesus knew what he was asking. The cost of God's grace severed relationships in his own home. He lived with sisters and brothers who thought he was "beside himself." Or as the New Revised Standard version translates this passage: "When his family heard it, they went out to restrain him, for people were saying, 'He has gone out of his mind' " (Mark 3:21). According to Luke, as a twelve-year-old, Jesus had said to his parents, "I must be about my Father's business" (Luke 2:49, adapting the KJV). A greater love was beckoning him beyond the perimeters of filial love.

Think of a mother who makes her son go to the teacher and admit that he does not deserve an A in the last examination because he cheated. Does she hate her son? Or think of the parents who accompany their son to the police station and urge him to confess his participation in a break-in at the music store. Do they hate their son? Or think of the wife who refuses to ride in the new car until her husband goes to the car dealer and admits that he had "doctored" up the engine in the car he traded in and then had lied when he said that it didn't burn oil.

Does she hate her husband? Or think of the husband who insists that his wife return to the dress shop the blouse which the sales clerk had mistakenly included in the bag containing her new dress. In all these instances, the love for Christ and his teachings appears to set family members against one another. A higher love prevails. Yet family love does not turn to hate; it only seems so.

At this point, for the first time, we may make a startling discovery. We truly love our children and spouse only when we love them in and through our love for Christ. To lie and cheat and cut corners and make unsavory compromises in order to protect our loved ones means to undermine character, destroy integrity, and betray honor. Yes, grace costs! But, O the frightening cost of "cheap grace"!

The late Paul Scherer, for many years a distinguished professor at Union Seminary in New York City, once told some of us about a painful injury suffered by a son. The child at play accidentally pierced his arm with a jagged piece of steel. Dr. Scherer rushed the child to a doctor's office. "We must remove that piece of steel at once," the physician observed. The son, though, resisted every effort which the doctor made. Finally, he turned to the father and said, "Help me pin your son down on the table. Put your weight on top of him and use whatever force it takes to hold both arms still." Dr. Scherer complied. He reflected on that moment: "I shall never forget the look in my son's eyes. It was a most hateful look, as though he were telling me, 'How could you do this to me? You say you love me, but you don't. You hate me!'" Scherer remarked, "Using force on my son and letting the doctor pull out that piece of steel and listening to my son's piercing screams of pain and seeing in his eyes that look of hate—that was the hardest thing I ever had to do."[17] Only later would the son realize that his father had allowed him to hurt so much because he so deeply loved him.

When we look at others through the eyes of God and love them in Christ's love, this is, compared to our love of God, a lesser love. Jesus goes so far as to name it "hate." This may be exaggeration, but the call to wholehearted commitment to God

is serious business. This is the grace that costs. But any other
way costs even more!

On Divorce, Remarriage, and Adultery
(Luke 16:18; Mark 10:11–12; Matt 5:31–32; 19:9)

Translation

> Everyone who divorces his wife and marries another commits adul-
> tery, and the one who marries a woman divorced from her husband
> commits adultery. (Luke 16:18)

> Whoever divorces his wife and marries another commits adultery
> against her,[18] and if she, after divorcing her husband, marries
> another, she commits adultery. (Mark 10:11–12)

> It was said, "Whoever divorces his wife, let him give her a bill of
> divorce." But I tell you, everyone who divorces his wife—except
> for the reason of illicit sexual behavior[19]—makes her an adulter-
> ess,[20] and whoever marries a divorced woman commits adultery.
> (Matt 5:31–32)

> Whoever divorces his wife—except for illicit sexual behavior[21]—
> and marries another commits adultery. (Matt 19:9)

An Interpretation

The church has long struggled with these stringent words
of Jesus on marriage and divorce. In fact, the apostle Paul was
already facing the pastor's challenge of interpreting and applying this teaching on divorce when he wrote 1 Corinthians (see
7:10–16; and cf. also Rom 7:2–3). If we leave out of consideration the exceptions allowed by Matthew, which probably served
to adapt Jesus' word to the specific needs of a Jewish Christian
community now welcoming gentiles,[22] and if we also set aside
the flexibility Paul shows in applying this "word of the Lord,"[23]
we come face to face with an uncompromising rejection of
divorce. This is another hard saying of Jesus, in our own time
just as surely as in his own.[24]

In order to understand Jesus' rigorous word on divorce, we must first be clear about the status of marriage and divorce in his culture and about the biblical tradition on which Jewish practice was built. Within the law of Moses, the principal piece of legislation concerning divorce is the very text used by Jesus in Mark 10:3–9 as a foil for his own position:

> Suppose a man enters into marriage with a woman, but she does not please him because he finds something objectionable about her, and so he writes her a certificate of divorce, puts it in her hand, and sends her out of his house; she then leaves his house and goes off to become another man's wife. Then suppose the second man dislikes her, writes her a bill of divorce, puts it in her hand, and sends her out of his house (or the second man who married her dies); her first husband, who sent her away, is not permitted to take her again to be his wife after she has been defiled; for that would be abhorrent to the Lord, and you shall not bring guilt on the land that the Lord your God is giving you as a possession. (Deut 24:1–4 NRSV)

It is clear that this passage assumes rather than creates norms governing the practice of divorce. It does not define acceptable grounds for divorce, simply mirroring, instead, the actual social convention. When the husband finds reason to be displeased with his wife, that is legitimate cause to send her away. The only point of the law is to prohibit the divorced woman's remarriage to her former husband. It is scarcely surprising that rabbis in Jesus' era would debate the legitimate grounds for divorce, *and* that they would find no real help in the Deuteronomy passage. But note a crucial feature of this text, which says a great deal about the reality of marriage in Jesus' culture: only the husband may initiate divorce,[25] and he may do so for reasons that range from weighty to frivolous.[26] There is little protection for women here (much less equal treatment under the law). And divorce, like the death of a husband, would make a woman particularly vulnerable, her future precarious at best. We should also point out that there is nothing in the Torah prohibiting polygamy; in fact, ample biblical precedent sanctions it.[27] Deuteronomy 24:1–4 even seems to reflect a practice of successive marriages that is virtually equivalent to polygamy. This was a not uncommon practice in Jesus' day. Once again, the woman can only be victimized in such a social arrangement.[28]

To summarize: the Jewish culture known to Jesus recognized divorce as a legitimate course of action *for men*, and no consensus existed concerning the appropriate grounds for divorce. Judging from two of the Dead Sea Scrolls, the strict discipline of the priestly community at Qumran may have prohibited divorce entirely.[29] That would, however, be the exception that proves the rule.[30] The right of a man to divorce his wife was widely accepted and practiced in first century Judaism. According to both Mark and Matthew, Jesus is drawn by antagonists into this arena of *halakic*[31] controversy: "Is it lawful for a man to divorce his wife?" (Mark 10:2; cf. Matt 19:3). Jesus' reply in Mark, treating the Mosaic provision of divorce as a mere concession to human sinfulness, presses beyond it to the divine intention for marriage from its inception:

> But from the beginning of creation, "[God] made them male and female." "Therefore a man will leave his father and mother and be joined to his wife, and the two will be one flesh." So they are no longer two, but one flesh. So then, let no one divide what God has united. (Mark 10:6–9 our translation)

Jesus deflects concern from escape clauses to an embracing of the unity of partners that reflects the creative design of God. How can a man cavalierly dismiss the woman whom God bound to him? And then we have the clincher: The man who does divorce his wife and then marries another is guilty of adultery. With one breath, Jesus affirms the sanctity and integrity of marriage as divine gift and denies its negation in divorce.

Why such a hard line against divorce? Was Jesus motivated by a concern for women who were the victims of divorce? Perhaps. Was he troubled by an all too casual treatment of marriage in his society? Perhaps. Did he even have the idea that all persons, not just priests, should live up to the vision of holiness prescribed in the Torah? (A priest was "holy to God" and therefore could not marry a divorced woman [Lev 21:7].) Perhaps. Whatever Jesus' motive, we are left with an ideal that is demanding, not to say impossible. We may hear ourselves in the voice of the disciples, according to Matthew: "If such is the case with a man and his wife, it is better not to marry" (19:10).

Has Jesus turned law-giver, seeking to impose an especially stringent law on his followers? Then would he insist that a man who remarries after divorce be put to death, as the law prescribes for adultery (Lev 20:10)? Would Jesus really claim that there are *no* circumstances when divorce is permissible, not even when a wife and her children are physically abused by the husband? Or is this, rather, another example of Jesus' characteristic use of exaggeration to challenge beliefs and practices which we take for granted? A hard saying to be taken seriously, but not to be pressed literally?

We should notice that Jesus does not *command* "no divorce." He does not say, "Thou shalt not divorce." Instead, the saying takes the form, "Whoever divorces and remarries commits adultery." The difference in form is significant.[32] Jesus forces us to re-examine our view of marriage by picturing in extreme imagery the consequences of its dissolution. We are shocked into seeing how much is at stake—what God has at stake—in marriage. God wills the joyous, mutually supportive partnership of husband and wife; in thwarting such a union, one undermines a relationship upon which God places immense value. Jesus, therefore, is using strong language to challenge a social arrangement that takes marriage lightly, and he does so to affirm marriage as a gift of God, a gift to be honored through enduring fidelity to one's partner.

We would contend, though, that Jesus has not authored a new piece of legislation, to be interpreted literally (divorce with remarriage equals adultery) and then applied (with perhaps some measure of flexibility, as Paul does in 1 Corinthians 7) to varying situations. No, Jesus' own acceptance of "sinners"—and they evidently included prostitutes and at least one woman caught in adultery[33]—suggests that persons who go through the wrenching experience of divorce would receive from him forgiveness rather than condemnation. It is crucial to keep this striking feature of Jesus' ministry in view; otherwise, we turn the "friend of tax collectors and sinners" into a harsh legalist.

It turns out, then, that we have responsible freedom in our response to this hard saying of Jesus, freedom to recognize situations of a different time and place in which divorce is preferable to continuing a marriage that bears no resemblance to the intimate bond Jesus has in mind. Freedom to think that while divorce is surely the result and reflection of human sinfulness, and while divorce is a tragic and painful transition, and while divorce-for-the-sake-of-marrying-another (more desirable mate) is unacceptable, nevertheless sometimes divorce is a step on the road to health, and sometimes remarriage after divorce is a sign not of sin but of wholeness.

Of course, we are in a way fighting against this hard saying of Jesus. We do so, however, not to diminish its power, not to evade its summons to responsibility and fidelity, not to weaken its affirmation of marriage, but rather to test its limits when it is understood as a statement of law. Nevertheless, one thing is beyond doubt. Genuine response to this word of Jesus, whether it comes from his first hearers or from us, must entail a deep respect (even an awed reverence) for marriage and a renewed commitment by marriage partners to "make it work," to nurture one's own marriage relationship with the loving care and fidelity and trust that mirror God's own care for us all.

From Text to Sermon: "Blest Be the Tie that Binds"

Friendship . . . love . . . courtship . . . marriage. This is what they say it used to be. But in these days, more than ever, it doesn't stop here. To this series, we have to add divorce. Some of you know this from personal experience. Marriages are made in heaven? Why then are some lived in hell? Broken marital relations affect over one-third of the marriages in the United States. We can no longer borrow and apply to weddings the first line of an old song: "Blest Be the Tie that Binds."

What Jesus has to say about marriage, divorce, and remarriage seems to make matters only worse. He sets marriage in the context of God's intent in creation. Two persons become "one flesh" in a union which cannot be dissolved. He says, "Whoever divorces his wife and marries another commits adultery against her, and if she, after divorcing her husband, marries another, she commits adultery" (Mark 10:11–12).

Why would Jesus hold to such a hard line? Look at Jewish history. The law of Moses opened the door for divorce: if a woman "does not please [her husband] because he finds something objectionable about her" he could prepare the divorce papers himself and send her away. The price he had paid for her (the dowry) was to be returned to her family. He was then free to marry someone else, as was she (cf. Deut 24:1–4). Followers of Moses through the centuries lowered the barriers so that almost any excuse could be used to justify divorce. Women, for the most part, were at the mercy of such a system. A woman was a piece of property, a thing.

The Greek world demanded fidelity of wives, but husbands were free to be promiscuous. Greek temples used prostitutes in the name of religion. Such practices influenced Roman culture, and undermined the home as the strong basis for Roman society. Even some Jewish contemporaries of Jesus succumbed to certain of these outside pressures.

In this context, Jesus sought to recover the sanctity of marriage and stem the flood of divorces. He saw around him shipwrecked homes, violence done to personhood, particularly to women and children. In such a setting he said: Those who divorce and remarry are committing adultery. Only this kind of teaching would get people's attention.

Even the disciples of Jesus reacted. They said that if this is the way it has to be, then it would be better never to get married! (Matt 19:10). And this is undoubtedly how many of you feel. People in every congregation have experienced broken marriages—their own or others'. They know that infidelity, physical or mental abuse, and severe incompatibility can make a life or a home seem like hell on earth. How can they and we live with these words of Jesus?

Matthew's version of what Jesus told his disciples suggests that Jesus, having gotten their undivided attention, softened the hard line. He said, "Not everyone can accept this teaching, but only those to whom it is given" (Matt 19:11). Was he implying that the highest ideal for marriage was beyond some people?

He went on to say, according to Matthew: "Let anyone accept this who can" (v. 12).

Further, it helps to see how Jesus treated adulterers. John's gospel relates that he did not shut the door of the kingdom on a Samaritan woman who had gone through five marriages and was living with a sixth man without benefit of marriage vows (see John 4:16–26).

When the scribes and Pharisees brought to Jesus a woman caught in the act of adultery, they challenged him to give the word from Mosaic law: death by stoning.[34] Jesus stooped down and made markings in the sand. Do you suppose that he was wondering why they had not also brought the man? He looked up and said, "Let anyone among you who is without sin be the first to throw a stone at her" (John 8:7). He then stooped down and made more tracings in the sand. And one by one the men went away. The older ones likely left first. They had lived longer, and probably remembered more sins, sins which at this moment they tried to cover with their shame. They who had come to condemn were gone. Jesus said to the woman (v. 11), "Neither do I condemn you. Go your way, and from now on, do not sin again."

When Simon the Pharisee entertained Jesus at a dinner party, he was greatly disturbed that Jesus allowed a sinner (woman of the street?) to bathe his feet with her tears, dry them with her hair, and anoint them (Luke 7:36–50). Jesus upbraided his indignant host, but had a message of mercy for the woman: "Your sins are forgiven . . . go in peace."

Both ancient hypocrites and we of the modern vintage are shamed by the words which the Master spoke one day: "But I say to you that everyone who looks at a woman with lust has already committed adultery with her in his heart" (Matt 5:28).

Jesus does not condone sin; he forgives the sinner. And to keep all hypocrites in their place, he said to some of them: "Truly I tell you, the tax collectors and the prostitutes are going into the kingdom of God ahead of you" (Matt 21:31). But dare we go on our way and not hear once more Jesus' words about marriage, divorce, and adultery as he speaks to our generation?

Sex is a three letter word, and it is spelled out across movie and television screens, magazine and book covers. Soap opera characters and nationally known preachers and politicians marry, commit adultery, divorce, and commit more adultery. In the protests of the 1960s they asked in song, "Where have all the flowers gone?" Today we ask, "Where have all the morals gone?"

A person once wrote to Ann Landers[35] reacting negatively to a television talk show in which a mother who was advocating abstinence from sexual intercourse by teens was shouted down. Mothers on the panel testified that they allowed their teens to have sex in their homes when the parents were present. In her reply, Ann Landers observed, in part, "As for standards of morality, forget it. That train left a long time ago."

Was it sex *with* or *without* love which Tennyson explored in "Locksley Hall"?

> He will hold thee, when his passion shall have
> spent its novel force,
> Something better than his dog, a little dearer
> than his horse.[36]

What can the local congregation do? What about sex education opportunities for our children and youth? What about the quality of our counseling for couples who come seeking to be married with the church's blessing? Can we not hold out to those trying to keep their marriages from falling apart a healing word in counseling that is based on the Christian faith? What do we have to offer the unwed pregnant girl? One out of every four children born in the United States today has an unwed mother, usually a teen. No child is illegitimate! The mother, and the father if he is found, are among those invited to Christ's wedding banquet. The Master who blessed and forgave the woman of the street who anointed his feet, the Lord who carried the little children in his arms, the Jesus who conversed with a Samaritan woman at the well in spite of his contemporaries' taboos, is calling us to go to life's byways and welcome people to the kingdom.

Love and marriage and sex are among God's greatest gifts. The commandment of long ago and the word of Jesus say the same thing: "You shall not commit adultery." But we are those who, if not in act, at least in mind and heart, are guilty. The penalty prescribed in the Pentateuch is death by stoning. None of us—men or women—can pay the cost which grace demands. But we see on the cross one who paid the price. He died not under the weight of stones but under the weight of all our sins, yours and mine. And when we see him there, we begin to understand the cost of grace.

Yes, we can see the cost of grace. The price Christ paid. But we cannot close till we have listened again to his call: "Friend, come up higher. Start climbing the Mt. Everest of love and marriage. Never be content with being average. The mediocre life is not for those who follow me. Be perfect, even as your Father in heaven is perfect." Our faith beckons us to sky-high ideals. In the words of Browning, "Ah, but a man's reach should exceed his grasp, Or what's a heaven for?"[37] Who would be satisfied with lower aim, any lesser purity or goodness or truth? For anything less would not be purity or goodness or truth!

SELF-ABUSE FOR THE SAKE OF THE KINGDOM?
(MARK 9:42–48)

Translation

> And whoever causes one of these little ones [who believe] to fall,[38] it would be better for such a one to have a millstone placed around his neck and to be thrown into the sea! And if your hand causes you to fall, cut it off! It is better to enter life maimed[39] than with two hands to depart to Gehenna, to the fire that cannot be put out.[40] And if your foot causes you to fall, cut it off! It is better for you to enter life lame[41] than with two feet to be thrown into Gehenna. And if your eye causes you to fall, take it out! It is better for you to enter the realm of God with one eye than with two eyes to be thrown into Gehenna, where "their worm does not die and the fire cannot be put out"[42] (cf. also Matt 18:6–9; Luke 17:1–2).

An Interpretation

F. F. Bruce remarks, in his discussion of this passage, that it has not been "recorded that anyone ever mutilated himself because of these words in the Gospels."[43] Surely no one would ever interpret *this* saying literally! Unfortunately, the authors personally know of one such tragedy, where a young boy lost his eye out of his church's "obedience" to Jesus' stern command. Like the word on hating parents, this text from Mark 9 is not only difficult but dangerous if misunderstood. The destructive potential of these sayings is obvious: does Jesus call for self-abuse for the sake of our participation in God's kingdom?

We must first distinguish between the first saying (a millstone around the neck) and the last three (removal of hand, foot, and eye). Mark 9:42 warns of the dangers attending a person who sets an obstacle before "one of these little ones,"[44] employing the graphic image of a large, heavy millstone around the neck to score the point. Better to die, even in such a grotesque manner, than to bring ruin to one such little one who enjoys the special favor of Jesus. The following three sayings, by contrast, warn of the consequences of setting an obstacle *before oneself*, and each of the three uses the arresting image of "Gehenna" to underscore the warning.[45] We turn now to the task of making sense of the last three sayings, which *seem* to advocate self-mutilation. What is Jesus' message here?

Each saying has a two-part structure. The first line advises the hearer to remove a part of the body that leads him or her to fall. The second line then gives the grounds for this warning: it is preferable by far to lose a part of the body than to forfeit life itself. We modern readers may be somewhat amused by the assumption that an eye or foot or hand is the cause of a person's destructive behavior. Of course, scandalous sexual behavior stems not from the eye but from the mind and self constituted as a whole; in the same way, a thief is not led to crime by his hand, nor is his escape motivated by his foot. And yet, the images Jesus has chosen are apt, are they not? The eye *is* the window of the lustful heart and the hand and foot *are* the servants of a violent spirit. And notice the strengthening of each image, with the adjective "right," considered in Jesus' culture to be the strong or powerful or good side. Even if it is one's "good" eye or hand or foot, it must be removed.

The commands are graphic: "Pluck it out!" "Cut it off!" "Cut it off!" Jesus certainly captures our attention with these shocking instructions. So also with the *worse* fate which Jesus would have his hearer avoid. It is far better to enter life, or the realm of God[46]—even with hand or foot or eye missing—than to find oneself in Gehenna.[47] Gehenna is actually the name of a valley on Jerusalem's south side (*Ge-ben-hinnom*), which had served, ever since the return from the Babylonian exile (6th century BCE), as the city's garbage dump and incinerator.[48] Eventually, this site, with its perpetual fires and terrible stench, came to provide a fitting symbol for the final destruction that awaited the wicked. Obviously, no one would wish to suffer that kind of torment, intensified even further by Jesus (according to Mark 9:48) through the gruesome scene, borrowed from Isa 66:24, of unceasing worms *and* fire.

Extreme language indeed! Extreme language because everything is at stake. Jesus has been sending out an invitation, and desires to welcome all into the joyous feast of God's reign. But in order to participate in the enduring life of the kingdom, the life of God, one must set aside every obstacle. Nothing else matters more; nothing else is more important; nothing else can be allowed to stand in the way. Not family or parents or possessions or security. No, and not the parts of one's body either—and that means *no aspect* of oneself. Once again, we meet exaggerated imagery, the point of which is that God's claim on my life transcends all other claims, that the supreme value of participating in the eternal blessing of God surpasses all other values, even good and noble ones. Eduard Schweizer has captured especially well the force of this hard saying of Jesus. Far from being an appeal for self-mutilation, this is

> a radical way of stating that it is more important to be obedient to God in all circumstances than it is to retain all the parts of the body intact. Nevertheless, the parts of one's body should not be despised; they are to be valued as [our] greatest treasure. . . . God is even more important than the most important parts of our bodies. . . . The objective is to free oneself from anything which might hinder fellowship with God.[49]

Clearly, this series of strong statements must not be taken literally, as if our place in God's realm really depended on body parts. But it is a sharp warning, to be received in utter seriousness, for nothing in my life is more important than my response to God's claim upon me—God's claim upon the whole of me and the whole of my life.[50] Our interpretation of Mark 9:42–48 has now brought us face to face with forceful language about *final judgment*. This language, too, poses a challenge for most modern readers. We tackle that challenge in chapter 3.

From Text to Sermon: "The Worth of a Soul, or Shall I Give My Body in Exchange for My Soul?"

Myra Brooks Welch, in her poem, "The Touch of the Master's Hand," says that

> the foolish crowd
> Never can quite understand
> The worth of a soul.[51]

One day Jesus asked, "What will a person give in exchange for his or her soul?" (Mark 8:36–37 our translation). He taught that life is precious, and that nothing is more important than the welfare and destination of the soul. He dramatized the worth of the soul with exaggerated metaphors: wearing a "millstone around the neck" and then being thrown overboard; cutting off the right hand or the right foot; plucking out the right eye (Mark 9:42–50). Such a fate, he said, would be better than causing another to fall or leading one's own self to fall. The first metaphor sounds like a tactic by the Mafia, and the second set of metaphors reminds one of horror stories coming out of the Middle East during the Persian Gulf War in 1991.

Let no one be mistaken. To take these sayings of Jesus in Mark 9:42–50 literally is to do a great injustice to the Bible and to misunderstand the spirit and teaching of Jesus. He spent much of his earthly ministry *healing bodies*. Self-mutilation had no place in his mission. When John the Baptist was in prison and wondered aloud about the confusing reports about Jesus that were coming to him, the Master, according to Matthew, sent this reply: "Go and tell John what you hear and see: the blind receive their sight, the lame walk, the lepers are cleansed, the deaf hear, the dead are raised, and the poor have good news brought to them" (Matt 11:4). Self-abuse? Jesus would have none of it. No one should take Mark 9:42–50 any more literally than they would the comment, "I would give my right arm to be in your place," or, "Go break a leg."

First, Jesus warns against the consequences of leading someone else astray. I am my brother's or my sister's keeper. I am held accountable if my words, actions, or attitudes lead another person to walk a lower road, descend to second-rate ideals, or slide down the road to hell. Jesus is not talking about the other person's culpability. That is between that individual and God. Jesus is talking, rather, about my liability. I am responsible when I cause another to fall. The judgment of time and eternity reveals the influence I have had, consciously or unconsciously, on the lives that crossed my path. Each one I have touched is either the better or the worse, the stronger or the weaker, the happier or the sadder, after she or he has moved on.

This is not to suggest that we become so entrapped in self-conscious, introspective mental fidgeting that we are like a centipede trying to decide which leg it must move next! The apostle Paul, in his letters to the churches at Rome and Corinth, counseled Christians how to handle the tension between one's own liberty and the conscience of another person. The issue at stake was whether or not to eat meat bought by the host at the market and labeled not as "prime choice" but as "from a sacrifice offered to an idol." Paul advised sensitivity to the conscience and spiritual welfare of the people at the dinner. To the Christians at Rome, he wrote, "Everything is indeed clean, but it is wrong for you to make others fall by what you eat; it is good not to eat meat or drink wine or do anything that makes your brother or sister stumble" (Rom 14:20–21 NRSV). In the same letter he reminded his readers: "We do not live to ourselves, and we do not die to ourselves" (Rom 14:7).

I thought of these words from Paul when, in the first church where I was pastor, a troubled father came to see me about one of his sons. The boy had struck and killed a pedestrian with his car while driving under the influence of alcohol. The father wanted me to visit his son in prison. Then he proceeded to tell me, "You know, I've been a social drinker through the years. I wanted to teach my boys how to handle their liquor. I gave them their first drink. How was I to know that Donnie would become an alcoholic?" I needed to say nothing. The cleansing that day was a flood of tears. I think that it made him feel better. But I knew that God's forgiveness could not lift all the burden from his heart. It was a kind of millstone around his neck.

Josiah Wedgewood, the renowned English potter of the eighteenth century, one day was showing a man and a youth through his factory. During the entire tour, the man used vile and offensive language and made lewd gestures. In the last room Mr. Wedgewood unlocked the door to a display cabinet and removed an exquisite vase. He pointed out its unique and expensive features. Then he lifted it above his head and dropped it on the floor. It broke into countless pieces. The man let out an oath and asked, "Why did you do that? I would have paid you anything you would have charged for such a vase." Wedgewood replied, "Sir, I can make another vase just like that one. But no one can replace what you have destroyed this day in the soul of this young man."

Our Lord does not want us to have to live with the scars which the arrows of our heedless, uncaring, and insensitive bows have left on others' lives—scars which remain long after the wounds have healed. And tragically some wounds never heal. Here we see another sign of the cost of grace.

Second, Jesus warns against our betrayal of our own life, the sale of our own soul for a mess of pottage. He says, "If your hand causes you to fall, cut it off! It is better to enter life maimed than with two hands to depart to Gehenna, to the fire that cannot be put out" (Mark 9:43). He makes the same point about an offending foot or eye. Cut it off! Pluck it out! Better to be crippled or blind than to be whole of body and thrown into Gehenna.

Lest anyone think that followers of Christ need not place a premium on the physical side of life, we call to mind what Jesus and the apostle Paul had to say on the subject. Jesus was sensitive to those conditions which threatened the welfare of the body. The miracle of the feeding of the five thousand may, on the deeper level, have pointed to him as the Bread of Life (as presented by John 6). But he fed the multitude because he had compassion on hungry people (see Matt 14:14–21). He taught his hearers that the God who fashioned the beauty of the lily and fed the birds of the air provided sustenance also for his people. He regarded a cup of water for the thirsty and food for the hungry as actions bearing eternal significance. He identified himself with those in need of food and drink. James Russell Lowell, in writing about the search for the holy grail, pens these lines about the knight's discovery when he gave a beggar some water from his battered cup and saw the cup transformed into the one Jesus drank from at the Last Supper:

> Who gives himself with his alms feeds three:
> Himself, his hungering neighbor, and me.[52]

The apostle Paul urged his readers in the church at Corinth to keep the body pure. He wrote, "Do you not know that your bodies are members of Christ? . . . Or do you not know that your body is a temple of the Holy Spirit? . . . therefore glorify God in your body" (1 Cor 6:15–20 NRSV).

It is crucial to set the passage about cutting off arm or foot and plucking out eye in the context of the high and holy regard for the body that meets us in both the gospels and the letters of the New Testament. Followers of Christ have seen him as the Great Physician, and have pioneered in the establishment of hospitals and clinics in scores of countries. The church has made the treatment and care of the body a central part of its mission. Indeed, the whole field of medicine owes an immense debt to the Christian church.

One of the ironies today is that on the one hand we are enamored with efforts to promote health and on the other hand we are battling forces that abuse and destroy the body. Calories, cholesterol, dieting, exercise, bodily fitness, warnings against tobacco and alcohol abuse, and the war against the use and distribution of illegal drugs are the talk of television shows and prime topics for newspapers and magazines. I heard of one chain smoker who commented, "I read so much about the dangers of cigarette smoking that I have made a big decision: I am going to give up reading!" At the same time that modern America is focused on physical health and body culture, we face a momentous onslaught by drug pushers and drug users. Countless children have been condemned to a life limited by severe mental or physical disabilities because the mothers who bore them were using cocaine or some other dangerous drug. On a different front, sexual promiscuity has contributed in large measure to the AIDS epidemic. It touches hundreds of thousands and leaves their bodies defenseless against disease.

In July of 1991, I watched a television interview featuring the former football great, Lyle Alzado. He had (and later died from) an inoperable brain tumor. He said frankly that his illness was the direct result of his heavy and long-term use of steroids. A few years ago, one of the most promising young basketball players drafted by the National Basketball Association, Len Bias, was fatally stricken. The autopsy revealed that his death was the result of the use of cocaine. Decades of alcohol abuse contributed to the early death of one of the nation's greatest sports heroes, Mickey Mantle. These tragic deaths illustrate the consequence of self-abuse. They shock the nation and sadden millions.

We need say nothing more to reinforce the importance of the body. But our generation, like most generations before us, is reminded by Jesus that the spiritual dimension of life—the soul—is even more precious in God's sight. The real "you" is what counts in time and eternity. This is why Jesus warned his followers, "Do not fear those who kill the body but cannot kill the soul; rather fear him who can destroy both soul and body in hell" (Matt 10:28 NRSV).

And this is why he uses the images of cutting off a hand or foot and plucking out an eye in order to save the soul. As pointed out in our interpretation above, the hand or the foot or the eye is not the instigator of evil but only the instrument of sin. When a boy throws a stone through his neighbor's window, neither the breaking of the glass nor the throwing of the stone is a sin. The sin is what lies in the mind of the boy, prompting him to throw the stone. What Jesus asks us to do is to purge the spirit, to operate on the evil vagaries of the mind, to do surgery on the soul.

Nothing is more important than this: to open the heart to the grace of God and let nothing keep us from entering God's kingdom. If discipline and sacrifice and cross-bearing seem too costly, we are urged to look into the Gehenna (the smoldering landfill) of endless misery, the hell of red-hot conscience, the awful experience of the absence of God. And perhaps, we hope and pray, this glimpse will save us from the unforgivable sin: saying a final and fatal "No" to God.

No hand or foot or eye needs to be sacrificed. The cost of such grace has been paid by the one who gave his all. Think of this when next you come to the Lord's Table and hear him say, "This is my body which is broken for you . . . this is my blood which is shed for you." Then you and I will know again the cost of grace.

A Final Reflection

We have seen in this chapter that Jesus makes the righteous uncomfortable with his acceptance of the undeserving, but he proceeds to make those who would follow him uncomfortable by demanding that they give up all for the sake of God's reign. The scandal of grace stems from Jesus' challenge to his opponents to acknowledge his work with "sinners." The cost of grace flows from his challenge to his disciples to live out of a radical, wholehearted commitment to God. Nevertheless, we assert the priority of grace in Jesus' ministry. Beatitude precedes the call to surrender all to God. In Jesus' work God's mighty rule is pressing relentlessly into the human story—with blessing for the helpless and hurting—*and therefore* we must surrender life in order to experience it again in all its joy and depth.

This chapter has been about the ultimate claim of God over human life, a claim from which there is no evasion. In wrestling with the cost of grace, already we have glimpsed images of a future judgment, held before Jesus' hearers to alert them to what is at stake. In the next chapter, we will discover difficult sayings of Jesus which trouble modern readers with the "offense of judgment."

For Further Reading

Harvey, *Strenuous Commands: The Ethic of Jesus.*
Eduard Schweizer, *The Good News according to Mark* (Atlanta: John Knox, 1970) 196–205.
Tannehill, *Sword of His Mouth.*

On Leaving the Dead to Bury the Dead:
Fitzmyer, *Gospel according to Luke*, 1.833–38.
Jack Dean Kingsbury, "On Following Jesus: The 'Eager' Scribe and the 'Reluctant' Disciple (Matthew 8.18–22)," *NTS* 34 (1988) 45–59.

On Divorce and Remarriage:
Bruce, *Hard Sayings of Jesus*, 56–62.
Raymond F. Collins, *Divorce in the New Testament* (Collegeville, Minn.: Liturgical, 1992).
Fitzmyer, *Gospel according to Luke*, 2.1119–24.
Fitzmyer, "The Matthean Divorce Texts and Some New Palestinian Evidence," in *To Advance the Gospel: New Testament Studies* (New York: Crossroad, 1981) 79–111 [more technical].
George W. MacRae, "New Testament Perspectives on Marriage and Divorce," in *Divorce and Remarriage in the Catholic Church* (ed. L. G. Wrenn; New York: Newman, 1973) 1–15.
Bruce Vawter, "The Biblical Theology of Divorce," *Proceedings of the Catholic Theological Society of America* 22 (1967) 223–43.

ENDNOTES

[1] A. E. Harvey, *Strenuous Commands: The Ethic of Jesus* (Philadelphia: Trinity Press International, 1990). Harvey provides an excellent discussion of the dimension of Jesus' message which we are addressing in this chapter. He situates Jesus within the tradition of Jewish wisdom

teaching (and, more broadly, the moral instruction of the Greco-Roman world), and he argues that the ethical teaching of Jesus "was not intended to provide a set of rules to regulate the moral conduct of his followers, but rather to challenge us to live 'as if' the kingdom were already a reality" (p. 210). Especially illuminating also is Robert Tanne-hill's *The Sword of His Mouth* (Philadelphia/Missoula: Fortress/ Schol-ars, 1975), a study of forceful and imaginative language in the sayings of Jesus which treats a few of the texts we explore here.

[2] Note also the specific elaborations of this command in Exod 21:15 ("Whoever strikes father or mother shall be put to death") and Exod 21:17 ("Whoever curses father or mother shall be put to death").

[3] Surely Matthew's leaner list of family ties is to be taken as illustrative rather than exhaustive, so that Luke's expanded list is appropriate, though neither necessary nor stylistically preferable (the addition of "wife" and "brothers and sisters" disrupts the rhythm of the original).

[4] Matthew and Luke also embed the saying in different narrative contexts. Matthew prefaces the saying on parents with one announcing familial and social divisions precipitated by Jesus' work (Matt 10:34–36), and places all these words about crisis within a great mission discourse to the disciples (Matthew 10). Luke, by contrast, includes the saying about father and mother in a section in which Jesus challenges the crowds following him to consider the cost of discipleship.

[5] The Greek verb for "hate" is *miseō*.

[6] We leave aside the first saying, Jesus' caution to a willing disciple that to follow him means to embrace homelessness. Matthew 8:19–22 includes this dialogue and the one revolving around burial, but not the third encounter narrated in Luke 9:61–62 (the "plow"). We should also note that in Matt 8:22 Jesus summons the potential disciple to "follow" him rather than bury his father, where Luke sets "proclaiming the reign of God" against the man's burial obligation.

[7] As expressed, for example, in Mishnah tractate *Berakot* 3.1: "One who is confronted by a dead relative is freed from reciting the *Shema*, from the Eighteen Benedictions, and from all the command-ments stated in the Torah." Other texts illustrating the importance of the duty to bury one's parents include Gen 50:4–6; Tob 4:3–4; 6:13–15; *Jub.* 23:7; 36:1–2, 18; *T. Reuben* 7:1–2; *T. Levi* 19:5.

[8] The relevant passages are Lev 21:1–3, 11; Num 6:6–7.

[9] For detailed treatments highlighting the radical nature of this saying, in which Jesus appears to call for disobedience to God's law, see Martin Hengel (*The Charismatic Leader and His Followers* [Edinburgh: T. & T. Clark, 1981]) and E. P. Sanders (*Jesus and Judaism* [Philadel-phia: Fortress, 1983] 252–55). Hengel's assessment (p. 14): "There is hardly a [saying] of Jesus which more sharply runs counter to law, piety, and custom than does [this one]."

[10] It is worth noting that Jesus fails to give a concession which, centuries before, the prophet Elijah had granted to Elisha (1 Kgs 19:19–21). Luke has crafted this scene in such a way that Jesus both stands in the tradition of Israel's great prophets and, at the same time, emerges as the pinnacle—the greatest prophet of all.

[11] Kenneth E. Bailey (*Through Peasant Eyes: A Literary-Cultural Approach to the Parables of Luke* [Grand Rapids: Eerdmans, 1980] 22–32) lays bare the cultural dynamics regarding family that sayings like Luke 9:59–62 presuppose. Bailey suggests that the phrase "to bury one's father" is an idiom expressing the son's duty to remain at home and care for his family until they are properly buried, and therefore that the man's father (in Luke 9:59–60) is not yet dead; rather, the potential disciple expects to return to his home and remain there until both his parents die. This explanation, while possible, is not necessary if we are dealing with an unusual, quite specific circumstance. On any reading, the clash between Jesus' claim and conventional roles and responsibilities is sharp.

[12] In a very brief discussion, Fred Craddock has captured this point especially well ("Luke," in *HBC*, 1028).

[13] This question will return in our discussion below of Mark 9:42–48. Robert Tannehill (*Sword of His Mouth*, e.g., 53–57) offers stimulating and particularly helpful reflections on Jesus' use of such forceful language.

[14] Martin Hengel (*The Charismatic Leader*, 13) finds the key to Jesus' provocative call to abandon family ties in the "motif of the destruction of the family" that will, according to many prophetic and apocalyptic writings, accompany the turmoil of the end-time (e.g, Mic 7:6; Zech 13:3; *1 Enoch* 99:5; 100:1–2; *Jub.* 23:16; and cf. also Mark 13:12 and Luke 12:53 [= Matt 10:35]). ". . . decision for Jesus does not bring peace but disruption . . . to families."

[15] *Webster's New Collegiate Dictionary* (Springfield, Mass., 1981).

[16] Gale Sayers, *I Am Third* (New York: Bantam Books, 1972); Earl Campbell with Sam Blair, *The Driving Force* (Waco: Word, 1980); Orel Hershiser with Jerry B. Jenkins, *Out of the Blue* (Brentwood, Tenn.: Wolgemuth & Hyatt, 1989); Nancy Lopez with Peter Schwed, *The Education of a Woman Golfer* (New York: Simon & Schuster, 1979); Tom Landry with Gregg Lewis, *An Autobiography: Tom Landry* (Grand Rapids: Zondervan, 1990).

[17] Related during a lecture at the Princeton Seminary Institute of Theology.

[18] Possibly "with her," that is, the second woman. The phrase is difficult: *epi autēn*, literally "upon her."

[19] The word is *porneia*, which may refer to a number of inappropriate sexual activities, including prostitution, adultery, or incest. Here the meaning must either be "adultery" or "illicit marital union," that

is, marriage within the degrees of kinship prohibited by Lev 18:6–18. As gentiles entered the Jewish Christian community of Matthew, the issue of already existing marriages within these kinship limits, permitted in pagan culture but forbidden by Jewish law, may have arisen. Hence Matthew's formulation of the exception "for reason of *porneia*." Divorce in such cases is permissible, Matthew holds. For a helpful, though somewhat technical discussion of this issue, see Fitzmyer, "Matthean Divorce Texts," esp. 87–88.

[20] Presumably when she remarries, although this is not stated. The parallel drawn with the man who marries a divorced woman (in the last part of v. 32) suggests that it is remarriage after divorce that is "adulterous." If so, this saying falls into line with Mark 10:11–12 and Luke 16:18, and also with Matt 19:9 (Matthew's revision of Mark 10:11–12).

[21] Again, the word is *porneia*.

[22] See n. 19 above.

[23] Although he clearly honors the "word of the Lord" forbidding divorce, Paul in 1 Cor 7:10–16 does permit divorce in the case of inter-faith marriages (that is, where one marriage partner had become a Christian and the other had not) and by extension, one might argue, in other circumstances where it is the only path to "peace" (v. 15). See the discussion by Victor Paul Furnish, *The Moral Teaching of Paul* (2d ed.; Nashville: Abingdon, 1985) 38–44.

[24] Divorce was commonplace in the Roman world, and to some extent also among Jews. The difference, however, was that according to Jewish law, only men could initiate divorce, while women also had this right in Roman law. Mark has clearly adapted Jesus' original saying to Roman custom when he extends its scope to encompass divorces initiated by women (Mark 10:12, not paralleled in the other gospels). Jesus' contemporaries, the purist priestly community at Qumran (whose legacy includes the Dead Sea Scrolls), strictly opposed divorce.

[25] The first century Jewish historian Josephus observes that the divorce initiated by Salome, sister of Herod the Great, ran counter to Jewish law, "for it is the man [alone] who is permitted to do this" (*Ant.* 15.7.10).

[26] Interpreting Deut 24:1–4, Josephus comments that a man "who wishes for whatever cause to be divorced from the wife who is living with him—and with mortals many such may arise—must certify in writing that he will have no further intercourse with her" (*Ant.* 4.8.23). The rabbinic debates concern how broad or narrow the permissible grounds for divorce should be.

[27] Although certainly the ludicrous extreme represented by Solomon, with his hundreds of wives (and foreign wives at that), is not meant as a model for emulation!

[28] It is therefore striking, by contrast, that the Torah's sanctions for adultery are even-handed, if harsh: the man and woman guilty of adultery are both to be killed (Lev 20:10). Recall that Jesus characterizes divorce and remarriage as tantamount to adultery. See the discussion in Harvey, *Strenuous Commands*, 82–89.

[29] See the discussion of 11QTemple 57:17–19 (the Temple Scroll) and CD 4:20–21 (the Damascus Document) in Fitzmyer, "Matthean Divorce Texts," 91–97.

[30] Note also the criticism of the practice of spurning an aging wife for a younger one in Mal 2:14–16 (cf. Prov 5:18), and the coupling of a positive view of marriage with a negative view of divorce in Sir 7:26; 36:24. Yet the wisdom tradition which meets us in Sirach grants, at the same time, that divorcing one's wife may be the right thing to do (Sir 25:26).

[31] That is, concerning *halakah*, the way one interprets and practices the Torah.

[32] See the helpful discussion by Tannehill, *Sword of His Mouth*, 95–98.

[33] According to John 7:53–8:11. Although this passage is lacking in some early manuscripts, is placed by other manuscripts in quite different gospel contexts (even—and more appropriately—in Luke's gospel), and accordingly does not belong in John's gospel, it does clearly preserve an early tradition of Jesus' conduct.

[34] See John 8:2–11. For the text-critical problem, see the previous note.

[35] *El Paso Times*, p. 3C, July 12, 1991.

[36] "Locksley Hall," in *The Poems and Plays of Alfred Lord Tennyson* (New York: Random House, 1938) 171.

[37] "Andrea del Sorte," in *The Selected Poems of Robert Browning* (New York: Walter J. Black, 1942) 185.

[38] The verb here is *skandalizō*, often translated "cause to sin." Our translation keeps closer to the literal force of the word. Note that Mark has assembled in this passage four sayings which all center on the dangers of causing another (v. 42) or oneself (vv. 43, 45, 47) to stumble and fall ("sin"). Each saying uses the verb *skandalizō*.

[39] There is a pleasing assonance in the Greek here: *kalon* ["better"] . . . *kyllon* ["maimed"].

[40] We omit vv. 44 and 46 (identical in wording to v. 48), which do not appear in many of the best early manuscripts and are likely a later addition.

[41] *Kalon* ["better"] . . . *chōlon* ["lame"].

[42] The quotation comes from Isa 66:24.

[43] Bruce, *Hard Sayings of Jesus*, 55.

[44] The additional phrase, "who believe" (missing from the parallel in Luke 17:2), makes it difficult to identify the "little ones" of whom

Jesus is speaking. In Mark 9:36–37 Jesus singles out a young child as the special target of his concern: "Whoever welcomes one such child in my name welcomes me, and whoever welcomes me welcomes not me but the one [God] who sent me" (v. 37). Yet 9:38–41 has Jesus express similar concern for disciples like John. Mark 9:42 appears, therefore, to combine the picture of "little ones" (i.e., children) from 9:36–37 and that of disciples (i.e., believers) from 9:38–41.

[45] Like Mark 9:42, however, each saying focuses on the dangers of placing an obstacle that causes one to fall (hence, bringing ruin), using the verb *skandalizō*. By the use of this "link word," Mark has tied together all four sayings.

[46] Which stands in for "life" in the culminating saying, Mark 9:47. The expressions "life" and "realm of God" here are to be taken as roughly synonymous; that is, Jesus has in view the joyous life of God's eternal realm.

[47] Unfortunately, often translated simply "hell" in some modern versions.

[48] An appropriate fate, one felt, for what had once been the locale where the worship of Molech was carried out.

[49] Schweizer, *Good News according to Mark*, 198–99.

[50] A point made repeatedly by Jesus using some variant of the saying, "Whoever seeks to preserve life will lose it; whoever loses life for my sake will keep it."

[51] In *The Touch of the Master's Hand* (Elgin, Ill.: Elgin Press, 1943) 12.

[52] James Russell Lowell, "The Vision of Sir Launfal," Part 2, stanza 8.

THE OFFENSE OF JUDGMENT

The gate is narrow and the road is
hard that leads to life, and there
are few who find it. (Matt 7:14)

WE HAVE SEEN THAT JESUS' MESSAGE OF THE EXTRAVAGANT GRACE
of God does not lead to "cheap grace" but to moral
seriousness of the highest order. Jesus issues a call, in fact, to
single-minded commitment to the ways of heaven. The teachings we explore in this chapter develop further the theme of
human responsibility. But what is a modern reader to do with
the stern language and imagery of *judgment*? It is time to
consider the offense of judgment in the message of Jesus.

THE SIN NOT FORGIVEN (MARK 3:28–29)

The passage concerning an "unforgivable sin" provides a useful
starting point, particularly because of the way in which it
affirms with remarkable clarity both the gracious mercy and
the searching judgment of God.

Translation

> *Truly, I tell you, people[1] will be forgiven all things, whatever sins*
> *and slanders they slanderously speak.[2] Yet whoever slanders the*
> *Holy Spirit does not have forgiveness forever, but is guilty of an*
> *eternal sin.*

An Interpretation

These are strong words! According to Mark, Jesus is responding to the accusations of opponents who label his exorcisms evil. He is able to coerce demonic powers, they allege, only because he is himself tapping evil power: "By the ruler of the demons he casts out demons" (Mark 3:22). This claim, Jesus counters, is absurd: why would the architect of evil adopt such a self-defeating strategy? No, those who look good in the face, who see God acting to restore health and selfhood to human beings, and who then call it evil, are beyond hope. Such willful resistance to the work of the holy God is inexcusable.

While Matthew anchors this hard saying of Jesus in the same polemical setting (Matt 12:31–32), Luke charts a different course. In Luke's gospel, this statement does not figure in the debate concerning Jesus' exorcisms (Luke 11:14–23) but in his appeal to the disciples to give bold testimony of him—even and especially in perilous times (Luke 12:10–12). One must rely on the Spirit of God to enable that courageous witness. Even so, for one whose courage fails and who therefore speaks a word against the Son of humanity (Jesus), there will be forgiveness.[3] Slander against the Holy Spirit, however, will not be forgiven.

What is slander (blasphemy) against the Spirit? Why are the stakes so high? Jesus affirms that the world is the place where God's powerful and empowering presence (Spirit) is encountered. It can be felt in a parent's forgiveness of a rebellious child, in a stranger's act of compassion, in the joyous embrace of one in need, or in the healing of the sick and troubled. But what if we refuse to discern the divine presence? What if we remain closed to God's gracious mercy? What if we are so adamant in our resistance to what is holy that we celebrate moral evil and condemn good? What then? Then we are the heirs of Jesus' critics in this story from Mark; we are slandering the Spirit of God. We close our lives, our very selves, to the renewing presence of the Spirit that alone can transform and save us.[4] How then can we recognize, much less respond to, the divine gift of forgiveness?

It should be clear that slander (blasphemy) against the Spirit of God is not to be understood as a single act or word or choice. If there has been such a moment in one's life, a moment about which one feels deep regret, it is clearly *not* the "eternal sin" but belongs to the "sins and slanders" that *are* forgiven. And that point reminds us of the other side of this hard saying of Jesus—its radical affirmation of the expansive mercy of God.[5] For if divine forgiveness can truly reach to touch every sin, except this one, then the divine graciousness is far beyond our imagining. Confronted with the gravity of this saying of Jesus concerning the sin not forgiven, one is astonished yet again by the extravagant mercy of God.

From Text to Sermon: "The Eternal Sin"[6]

Matthew, Mark, and Luke all include passages about what is generally named "the unforgivable sin." The very term is frightening. It seems to point to what William Clow in a different context called "the dark line in God's face."[7] Halford E. Luccock, in his exposition of this passage in Mark, aptly suggests that some would assign it to the category of "things I wish Jesus had never said."[8]

First, let us look at this hard saying of Jesus in its canonical context. Both Matthew and Mark set the unforgivable sin in the encounter between Jesus and those who attribute his miracles to his use of demonic rather than divine power. Luccock likens their comments to the perspective of John Milton's Satan: "Evil, be thou my good."[9] They deny the presence and power of God in the word and work of Jesus, and so they slander or blaspheme the Holy Spirit. Those who will later charge Jesus with blasphemy (a sin punishable in their law by death) here blaspheme the Holy Spirit—God's reality and presence in the world.

Luke refers to the unforgivable sin in a way that would speak directly to the precarious situation confronting many early Christians in the Roman Empire. Because Christians (like Jews) believed in only one God and refused to worship the many other gods and goddesses of the day, the Romans thought that they were atheists. Bold witness would be needed by Jesus' followers in an alien and unfriendly world. The time would come when many of them would be commanded to bow down before the image of the Roman Emperor. To refuse to do so would mean death. My own belief is that Jesus was implying, "I won't hold it against you if you slander my name. I shall understand and forgive you. But if in your heart you deny God, you are slandering the Holy Spirit. That sin cannot be forgiven."

In all three gospels Jesus is quoted as saying all sins will be forgiven, including slander against Jesus himself, but the slander against the Holy Spirit never has forgiveness. When Jesus later was to pray from the cross, "Father, forgive them; for they do not know what they are doing" (Luke 23:34), there would be one sin not included in the dispensation of mercy. You can slander and even kill me and still receive mercy, but you dare not ultimately reject God. This would be an unrelenting refusal to have anything to do with God. This would be unforgivable. Peter would deny Jesus with a curse, and he would be forgiven. And so the mercy would flow abundantly for him and for us in our sin. But let no one close life forever against God.

Countless people have worried and agonized because they think that they have committed an unforgivable sin. Let them cheer up and even smile through their tears. For anyone who is so troubled has not committed the eternal sin. The person who slanders the Holy Spirit does not worry about it. Such a one has opted to place life beyond the reach of redemption. Such a person has allowed the heart to harden like concrete and has closed life to the reality and presence of God.

I once heard a story about a boy who was excited when he heard that the circus was coming to his town. He watched as the main street was paved with concrete just prior to the arrival of the circus. Like some of his friends he had sneaked out to make an indentation with his bare foot in the freshly laid cement. (Did you ever put a finger near a "fresh paint" sign, or make a mark with your finger near the "fresh cement" notice?) This boy made his mark. Then the circus came to town. Main Street was the route of the parade. Along came the wagons with the caged lions and tigers. At last came the huge elephants, lumbering along the pavement. The boy, remembering the print of his foot in the concrete, rushed out after the elephants passed, eager to see the footprints of the elephants. But there were no marks! The concrete was now impervious even to the weight of mighty elephants. This is a parable of the hardened heart. Even God cannot make a mark within such a heart.

God never forces himself upon us. Holman Hunt painted two identical portraits of Christ called "The Light of the World." One hangs in Keble College at Oxford, England, and the other in St. Paul's Cathedral in London. These paintings show Christ, holding a lantern, standing at the door of an ivy covered cottage. One notices that there is no latch on the outside of the door. The door can be opened only from the inside. This is a visual parable. God comes through the Spirit in countless ways in this world to offer himself for our wholeness and well-being. But Jesus does not force or break open the door. He waits till the door is opened from within. He says, "Listen! I am standing at the door, knocking; if you hear my voice and open the door, I will come in to you and eat with you, and you with me" (Rev 3:20 NRSV).

God made us with the power of choice. We are free to say "Yes" to God, or to say "No." Indeed, this manifests the extreme to which God dared to go in creating us to become either his greatest friends or his most bitter enemies. God even allows us to "play god" and to be his rivals, if we so choose. This began to be apparent in the saga of the Garden of Eden when our first parents defied God's lone "Thou shalt not," and ate the forbidden fruit.

This is the guarantee of our freedom: we can will to reject God by what we think and what we say and what we do. Hereby we indicate to God that we do not want to have anything to do with him. "Hell" is the guarantee of that freedom. It is as though God were saying, "I would like you to come to me and walk with me, but I will not make you do it. If you choose to go the other way, you are free to go. You are free to go to hell!"

The unforgivable sin, therefore, is to refuse—to our dying breath—to have anything to do with God. God will receive us even at the last moment, if we change our minds. The proof of this is the case of the thief on the cross beside the cross of Jesus. He said, "Jesus, remember me when you come into your kingdom." And Jesus answered, "Truly, I tell you, today you will be with me in Paradise" (Luke 23:42–43 NRSV). Yet only one of the two thieves there said "Yes" at the last moment. And so we dare not presume too much or wait too long.

To blaspheme or slander the Holy Spirit simply means to refuse to have anything to do with God. This is the ultimate, the final "No." This is the eternal sin.

Does this not fall like a warning shadow across the countless multitudes in our secular age? They may not deny the existence of God, but they live as though the reality of God's presence in the world does not matter. We may call it "living on the edge."

In a later part of this chapter on "The Offense of Judgment," we shall come face to face with the other side of the unforgivable sin: the rejection of God through the rejection of one's neighbor. Let it suffice here to say that Jesus in his teaching and the New Testament in its reflections on judgment and mercy state in stark terms the connection between God's forgiveness and our forgiveness of others. We shall see how the life that closes itself to another human being nullifies the possibility of receiving God's mercy.

As the debates rage in our day over the issues of abortion, homosexuality, and the use of public tax dollars for feeding the hungry and sheltering the homeless, we are reminded that in an earlier day the church opposed efforts to extend rights to women and to protect the welfare of women and children in the sweatshops and unsafe coal mines. And what of the long silence of the church in the rape of the earth, the polluting of the environment, and the poisoning of the air and water? Christians, above all others, are called upon to ponder what we call "evil" and what we call "good." For ours, too, is the temptation to slander God. Let us pray that we may become more sensitive, more aware of God's word, God's will. When God speaks, do we hear? Can we retain our sense of sin? Do we recognize the demonic and the divine?

We speak this further word to help us cope with the offense of judgment. A man called Saul was the archenemy of Jesus in the early days of the church. He slandered the Holy Spirit. According to the Acts of the Apostles, he consented to the martyrdom of Stephen. He persecuted other Christians with vehemence. But before it was too late, he saw the light, and he received everlasting mercy. When you read about Paul, you see that it is possible for anyone to change and be changed. Yes, there is hope for you and me. And so we sing, "Amazing grace, how sweet the sound that saved a wretch like me."

For Further Reading

M. Eugene Boring, "The Unforgivable Sin Logion Mark III 28–29 / Matt XII 31–32 / Luke XII 10: Formal Analysis and History of the Tradition, *NovT* 18 (1976) 258–79 [more technical].

Fitzmyer, *Gospel according to Luke*, 1.962–67.

Schweizer, *Gospel according to Mark*, 84–87.

ON BEING LEFT OUT AT THE FINAL BANQUET
(MATT 22:1–14; LUKE 14:16–24)

Jesus was evidently notorious for his festive meals, especially for his poor taste in selecting meal companions. Indeed, he was sharply criticized for his willingness to enter into the intimacy of the shared meal with "tax collectors and sinners" (e.g., Mark 2:16; Luke 7:34; 15:2). Yet in those meals (as also in Jesus' healing of the sick and disabled) something of the reality of heaven had broken into the pain and brokenness of human life. The meals expressed tangibly, though only by way of anticipation, the festive communion of heaven. It is no surprise, then, that Jesus seizes upon the banquet as an apt image of the joy and graciousness of the realm of God. Anyone and everyone are invited to come to this table. There is, however, a darker side to this imagery. Only those who accept the invitation actually enjoy the meal, a point Jesus drives home with his parable of a banquet in which the invited guests fail to appear and forfeit their places to others. Like the saying concerning the sin not forgiven, this parable ties together the themes of mercy and judgment.

The parable appears in quite different forms in Matthew and Luke.[10] Luke presents a "certain man" hosting a banquet (a "great dinner"). A rather ordinary occasion becomes quite extraordinary, however, when all the invited guests dishonor the host by declining at the last moment to attend the banquet. In Matthew, though, the dinner turns into a wedding banquet celebrating the marriage of a king's son. Expressions of contempt and acts of violence escalate in Matthew's account of the parable, which includes the king's revenge (the destruction of a rebellious city) and culminates in the enigmatic expulsion of a guest not dressed for so grandiose an occasion.[11]

Although Jesus may well have told this parable with significant variations in different settings, the embellishments in Matthew appear to reflect Israel's experience of catastrophe in the year 70 CE, when the rebellion against Rome resulted in the fall of Jerusalem and the destruction of the second temple. So the parable comes to offer a retrospective on this painful chapter in Jewish history; it provides a theological explanation for the fall of the holy city. Having treated with cruelty and contempt the "King's" son (Jesus), the city was ripe for judgment. Matthew, then, reshapes the parable of the banquet to address the experiences and concerns of his audience in the last part of the first century. None of these allegorizing elements, however, are present in Luke's version of the parable, which surely resembles more closely than Matthew's the original structure of the story. Accordingly, we will focus our study on Luke 14:16–24.

Translation

> A certain man had a great dinner, and he invited many people. At the hour of the dinner, he sent his servant to say to those who had been invited, "Come, for it is now ready." And they all began, one by one, to ask to be excused. The first said to him, "I bought a field, and I need to go and see it. I ask you, have me excused." And another said, "I bought five teams of oxen and I am going to inspect

them. I ask you, have me excused." Yet another said, "I married a woman, and so I cannot come."

Now when the servant returned, he reported these things to his master. Then the owner of the house became angry and said to his servant, "Go out quickly into the streets and alleys of the city, and bring back here the poor and crippled and blind and lame." And the servant said, "Master, what you commanded has been done, and there is still room." And the master said to the servant, "Go out onto the roads and byways, and compel [them] to come in, so that my house may be filled. For I tell you, none of those men who had been invited will taste my dinner."

An Interpretation

It should have been a grand evening. Invitations to the banquet had been sent and, it is quite clear, accepted. As with all such festive occasions, the dinner would afford the host the opportunity for an impressive display of generosity to his peers among the important men of the town. With their enjoyment of the meal would come honor and praise for their host. No prize was more coveted than honor from one's peers.

How the tables have turned! When the dinner is prepared, according to custom the host dispatches his servant to summon the guests to his home. Yet, at the last minute, they refuse to come, every last one of them. It is as if the invited guests had conspired to snub the host. To be sure, they politely request to be excused, and each justifies his breach of etiquette with an explanation. But are these legitimate excuses? "I bought a field, and I need to see it." Will the field still be there tomorrow? "I bought five teams of oxen [ten oxen in all], and I am going to inspect them." As if he had undertaken such an investment sight unseen! "I just got married, so I can't come." Really? Then why aren't all of us at the wedding celebration? These weddings are long planned and eagerly awaited by everyone—they are on every calendar in town! It appears, therefore, that each of these excuses is . . . well, inexcusable.[12] As with one voice, dinner guests who had previously accepted the invitation to attend a wonderful banquet have now shown contempt for the host.

No wonder he becomes angry! Of course he will get back at them. But notice the form his revenge takes. He hastily compiles a new guest list, and he starts in the most unimaginable place, with all the socially marginal persons in the town—the poor and those with various physical disabilities. Our host's generosity will not be denied, and he flavors it with humor as well. He ensures that he will receive honor tonight, even if it must come from people of such low status. At least *they* will be grateful!

Naturally, they come, although the narrator of the parable (Jesus) mentions neither the servant's search nor the new guests' arrival. As hearers of the parable, we easily fill that "gap" in the story. Meanwhile, though, our attention is riveted on the important issue, namely the host's response to his dilemma. And he still has a problem on his hands. The banquet hall is not yet full. What if some from the original guest list decide to show up late? The host wants a full house, but there is no room here for the ungrateful. Therefore, a now weary servant is sent to the roads outside the town to find . . . just anybody. "Compel them to come in." What sense can we make of that order?[13] The host is intent on filling his house with people. Yet could a stranger be expected to accept such a sudden and strange invitation? Would even someone who knows the host, but who is of lower social rank, dare to come? Of course not. The force of the command, then, is simply this: the servant is to take these folks by the arm and bring them to the banquet, for otherwise they would certainly—not realizing that they are truly wanted—decline to come. In other words, having been shunned enough times for one day, the host *will not take no for an answer.*

What is Jesus' message in this arresting story? Surely the parable paints in vivid colors a picture of the astonishing, inclusive grace of God, the theme we explored in chapter 1. We meet here Jesus' image of the realm of God as a great feast where there is room for anybody and everybody. Within the setting of Jesus' public ministry, that would mean, in particular, the "last, the lost, and the least" among the Jewish people—the poor, the sick and disabled, and the "sinners." These persons living on the margins of the community have responded to Jesus' teaching and healing; they have accepted his invitation into the family of God.

The last word of the parable, however, is not about grace but judgment: "I tell you, none of those men who had been invited will taste my dinner." There is, finally, no way of compelling people to say "yes" to God's gracious invitation. Jesus, with his meals, his words, his acts of healing, is opening up access to God's realm. Yet for those who resist and oppose his work, there is a sharp warning. People who feel quite confident of their place in God's house run the risk of locking themselves out of the greatest party of all. By denying *his* invitation to fellowship, they are denying life's most important invitation! Everything is at stake, and now is the time to come. This is no time for deferred decisions. The logic of this story implies the reality of divine judgment, tied inextricably to the reality of divine grace (generosity). The joy of heaven is for all who will embrace it, but at the same time God's home is no place for someone who would rather not be there.

From Text to Sermon: "The Men Who Didn't Come to Dinner"

A West Texas newspaper carried a story under the headline, "Woman Literally Crashes Party." It read: "A 34-year-old woman crashed a party on Avenue L Thursday night—literally. She drove a 1977 Cadillac into the front porch after being told she wasn't welcome, police said."[14] The police found the car parked on the front porch of the house in which the party was being held.

The host of the party in Lubbock had a problem directly opposite to that of the host of the great dinner in one of the parables told by Jesus. This man, when the last-minute details were completed and the time of the dinner arrived, sent out his servant (as was the custom) to summon all the people who had previously accepted invitations to the dinner. Every one of them had an excuse for not coming, and sent back word, "I ask you, have me excused."

The host of what was to have been a great dinner was very angry. He told his servant that none of those who had been invited would be admitted even if they showed up late. He said, "Go out quickly into the streets and alleys of the city, and bring back here the poor and crippled and blind and lame." When this was done and the guests had come, the servant reported that there still were some empty couches. The host told the servant to go back out into the roads and byways and take people by the arm and bring them in. The host wanted a full house!

According to Luke, when Jesus told this parable he was a dinner guest in the house of a leading Pharisee. As Jesus looked around at his fellow guests, apparently he noticed that they were the prominent citizens of the city: those listed in the city's social register, the business tycoons, the wealthy neighbors. He must have smiled—or grimaced—as he saw the guests vying for the places of honor. He told them that it was less embarrassing to take a lower place and be moved up than to choose a higher place and be moved down.

Then he turned to the host and said (perhaps in whispered tones?) that for his next big banquet he should skip these people and invite, instead, "the poor, the crippled, the lame, and the blind" (Luke 14:13). If you are buying favors by hosting these guests who are reclining on your couches, try inviting those who can't pay you back because they are too poor and live in houses too small to hold a banquet.

One of the dinner guests evidently overheard the conversation and blurted out, "Blessed is anyone who will eat bread in the kingdom of God!" It was in the silence which followed this exclamation that Jesus told the story of the great dinner to which none on the original guest list came.

Yes, blessed are those who will eat bread at God's banquet table. But God's guest list is shockingly different. It does not include those who take for granted that they deserve to be invited. It does not include those who are so casual about being in God's favor that they put everything else before dinner in God's house. Their excuses for neglecting God's invitation are as flimsy as the ones mentioned in Jesus' story. One had bought a new piece of land, and reported that he had to go to take a look at it. No, he did not have to take a look at it. He already had checked it out carefully before he bought it. He was too shrewd to buy land sight unseen. One had bought five teams of oxen; he sent word that he had to go inspect them. Did he buy ten oxen without looking at them first? Of course not. They cost him a lot of money. He would have checked them out carefully: their age, their condition, their disposition. And then there was the new bridegroom. Weddings in those times lasted for days. The host of the dinner would have been there if he had been invited, but the host apparently had not been on the guest list for the wedding. Though the excuse for the newlywed was better than those of the other two men, in that day and culture the excuse was poor at best. Don't lose sight of the fact that all of them had accepted invitations earlier.

Excuses! Someone said that when one does not have a good reason, a poor excuse is better than none. But Jesus was talking about God's great dinner, the so-called Messianic Banquet—the celebration of God's victory, the coming together of sinners transformed into saints by the grace of God. And yet those who take for granted that they deserve to attend and can come and go on their own time schedule—even expect places of honor—so clutter up their lives that they forget, they forget! When the day of the banquet comes and God's servant appears with the announcement that the hour has arrived, they make excuses and send their regrets.

Too late! The "ins" are out, and the "outs" are in. For, as Jesus told a hypocritical audience of his contemporaries, "Truly, I tell you, the tax collectors and the prostitutes are going into the kingdom of God ahead of you" (Matt 21:31 NRSV). Again, we are offended by God's judgment—and by God's grace.

Those of us who consider ourselves to be the respectable and righteous segment of society resent any intimation that we are not God's favorites. We can hardly conceive that "the dregs of society" are on any divine invitation list.

But human measuring sticks and human tests of merit have no relevance to God's requirements for admission to the kingdom. We would do well to remember this when we picture what the church—the earthly model of God's realm—ought to look like. In the earlier days of the struggle to remove the barriers of race and ethnic origin from the entrances of the church, one church elder was livid with anger when a black person asked for admission to the church. The elder shouted, "I'll not allow any black person to belong to my church." The pastor replied, "*your* church? But this is not *your* church. This is *Christ's* church."

The apostle Paul, more clearly than the original apostles, caught the vision of Jesus: an inclusive fellowship which beckoned welcome to the gentile world. This was so offensive to Paul's own people that he was hounded from city to city by his detractors. The kingdom, he insisted, was for Greeks and slaves and women, and not just for Jews and free people and men.[15]

We catch a glimpse of the shocking nature of God's realm when we see ourselves on the fringes. We very well may be the ones on the byways and back alleys. We are the sinners.

I paraphrase Paul Lawrence Dunbar's poem, "The Little Black Sheep":

> Poor little black sheep which strayed away,
> All lost in the wind and the rain—
> And the Shepherd says, "O hireling,
> Go find my sheep again."
> And the hireling says, "O Shepherd,
> That sheep is bad."
> But the Shepherd smiles, like that little black sheep
> Was the only lamb that He had.
>
> And the Shepherd went out in the darkness
> Where the night was cold and bleak,
> And that little black sheep, He finds it.
> And lays it against His cheek.
> And the hireling frowns, "O Shepherd,
> Don't bring that sheep to me!"
> But the Shepherd smiles, and holds it close.
> And—that little black sheep—was—me![16]

Yes, this is the judgment and the grace. That little black sheep was "me." And you.

For Further Reading

Bailey, *Through Peasant Eyes*, 88–113.
Breech, *Silence of Jesus*, 114–41.
Donahue, *Gospel in Parable*, 140–46.

Fitzmyer, *Gospel according to Luke*, 2.1048–59.
Marshall, *Commentary on Luke*, 584–91.
Scott, *Hear Then the Parable*, 161–74.

WHEN MERCY FAILS: THE PARABLE OF THE UNFORGIVING SERVANT (MATT 18:23–35)

Perhaps no saying of Jesus so clearly articulates the close connection between divine grace and divine judgment as does the
parable of the forgiven yet unforgiving servant.

Translation

> *The realm of heaven is like a man—a king—who wanted to settle
> accounts with his slaves. When he began to do the accounting, one
> was brought to him who owed him ten thousand talents. But since
> he was not able to pay, the master gave the order that he be sold,
> together with his wife and children and everything he owned, and
> that payment be made. So the slave fell down to his knees before
> him and said, "Be patient with me, and I will pay you everything."
> And that slave's master was moved to compassion, and let him go,
> and he forgave him the debt.*
>
> *When that slave went out, however, he found one of his fellow
> slaves who owed him a hundred denarii. He seized him and began
> to choke him, saying, "Pay what you owe!" So the fellow slave was
> pleading with him, "Be patient with me, and I will pay you." But
> he was not willing; instead, he went out and threw him in jail until
> he repaid the debt. Therefore, when his fellow slaves saw what had
> happened, they were greatly upset, and they came and reported to
> their master everything that had occurred. Then [the slave's] mas-
> ter summoned him and says[17] to him, "Wicked slave, I forgave you
> that whole debt, since you pleaded with me. Wasn't it incumbent
> upon you, too, to show mercy to your fellow slave, just as I showed
> mercy to you?" And in anger his master handed him over to be
> tortured until he should repay the entire debt.*

An Interpretation

This is not the first time the themes of debt and forgiveness have appeared together in Matthew's gospel. The model

prayer taught by Jesus in the sermon on the mount includes this petition: "Forgive us our debts, as we also have forgiven our debtors" (6:12). Jesus reinforces that petition in even stronger words at the close of the prayer: "For if you forgive others their trespasses, your heavenly Father will also forgive you; but if you do not forgive others, neither will your Father forgive your trespasses" (6:14–15). The parable of the unforgiving servant is a dramatic illustration of this challenging saying. If one expects to receive forgiveness, then one had better be in the forgiving business, too!

Matthew sets the stage for the parable with a conversation between Peter and Jesus concerning the limits of forgiveness. We can only admire the generous spirit of Peter. After all, doesn't a willingness to forgive a person seven times represent more than enough mercy for one relationship? Jesus, though, urges us to throw out the calculators ("seventy-seven times" or "seventy times seven") and keep on forgiving. That is to say, forgiveness, like love, has no limits (recall the parable of the good Samaritan). But why? The ensuing parable suggests an answer: we forgive and go on forgiving because we have ourselves been forgiven by God.

There is nevertheless an intriguing tension between the parable and this opening conversation between Jesus and Peter. The king in the parable surprises us with his nearly unlimited mercy (ten thousand talents): an apt image of God's mercy. Yet the king does not forgive as many as seven times, or even two. If the king in the parable images God for us, is God really less forgiving than we are expected to be? Are there, in fact, limits to forgiveness? We need to study the parable more closely.

The plot of the story unfolds in three stages: (1) a debt is canceled; (2) a second debt is retained; (3) the first debt is reinstated. The central character in the parable is the unforgiving servant, who receives mercy from his master (the king), but then refuses mercy to a fellow slave. The parable ends with the unforgiving servant's demise. A story that might have ended in joyous celebration of the unexpected generosity of the master—a movement from death to life—takes instead a tragic turn, leaving the "hero" of the tale without hope.

The comparison of these two situations of debt is revealing. The first slave owes his master ten thousand talents, the equivalent of several million dollars.[18] The reader may presume that the slave is a highly placed government servant who is charged with considerable responsibility for financial affairs in the kingdom.[19] Only with great responsibility could one amass such an immense debt. Whatever the explanation of the debt,[20] the reader anxiously observes as the slave enters a moment of grave crisis. The king opens the books and calls for full payment of the debt. When the slave is unable to pay, the king proves himself to be hard-hearted and predictable (or so it seems). He will have the slave and his family, along with their possessions, sold. It is strictly business, one might say. At least in this way the master will recover a small portion of the debt. The slave, though, appeals for mercy; he asks for an extension. Then comes the shock: the master/creditor does not give extra time but cancels the debt entirely. This is an unbelievably generous act. How will the servant respond?

He immediately accosts another slave who owes him one hundred denarii, a modest debt corresponding to a few weeks' wages, and demands payment.[21] Notice that the debtor repeats, almost word for word, the plea for mercy that the first servant had used so successfully with his master. "Just be patient with me, and I will repay you." Now it is the forgiven servant's turn to surprise the reader. No forgiveness here! Not even an extension. The debtor is sent to jail until he can repay. The beneficiary of extravagant mercy now insists on strict justice.

But *is* this justice? Not according to the other slaves who observe the events! This is anything but fair and right, and so they report everything to the king. The forgiven but unforgiving servant is summoned and the voice of the king expresses the point of the parable: "Wasn't it incumbent upon you to show mercy to your fellow slave, just as I showed mercy to you?" Therefore the unforgiving servant is sent to the jailers, who will make his life quite unpleasant until he repays the debt. Given the size of the debt, that day will surely never come. If the slave wants to insist on strict justice, then he certainly gets what he deserves.

It is a vivid and memorable tale. The message and appeal of the parable are clear enough: those who receive mercy are expected to extend mercy to others. Or put in theological language: we have been forgiven by God; it is now incumbent upon us to forgive others. Two problems, however, still remain. First, how can we make sense of the unforgiving servant's actions? How could he do this? Second, if the king in the story in some way represents God, what are we to do with the king's abrupt turn away from mercy?

How could the servant experience grace and respond as he does? We may better understand his reaction if we view the story with an eye to the cultural value of *reciprocity*, such an important value in Jesus' social world. If someone shows kindness or gives a favor or gift to me, then I am obligated to return the kindness or give honor or another valued gift to that person in exchange.[22]

The transaction in our parable concerns a master and his slave. The master's generous act of kindness ironically creates a new kind of debt on the part of the servant, who no longer owes his master the canceled debt but now does owe gratitude, honor, and in the future ever more loyal, diligent, and effective service. Yet this transaction touches only these two parties—or so the forgiven servant assumes. *No obligation follows in relation to other persons.* Clearly the servant acts on that assumption, only to discover, to his dismay, that the generosity he had received from his master really should extend to his relationships to other people.[23] The kindness from which I have benefited should reach to touch others who had no part in that original act of kindness. Since, in the parable, the king in some way embodies the graciousness of God, the point is that I should be so transformed by the experience of divine grace that I am able to bring that same grace and mercy into all my relationships with others. As Eduard Schweizer so aptly puts it, "God's forgiveness is not for decoration but for use."[24]

This line of reflection raises, though, the difficult question whether or to what extent the character of the king in the story expresses the character of God.[25] We would be wise not to press the details too far. Certainly the king's extraordinary and unimaginable act of mercy is to be seen as a reflection of divine grace. And just as surely, the experience of that divine grace should and must lead us to extend mercy to others. The one forgiven—who knows deep within both the depth of sin and the reality of grace—ought to be less prone to condemn the other. So the note of warning on which the parable closes should not be taken lightly. Yet it would be a mistake to insist that God will act in precisely the same fashion as this king, who shifts so easily from harsh demand to remarkable kindness and then back again. God is not so capricious! Still, the challenge addressed by this parable to the reader is clear and unavoidable. We who have been forgiven must now forgive.

If for no other reason, this is a genuinely hard saying of Jesus because forgiveness is itself so difficult. Trivial slights are easy enough to forgive. But when you have been badly hurt by another, especially—as seems to be so often the case—by those closest to you, mercy does not come easily. There is deep hurt and anger to be addressed, and injury to a relationship to be mended. Of course, genuine forgiveness can come only with time, and not by overlooking or simply forgetting the injury. Rather, one must take it seriously and acknowledge the depth of the hurt and of the anger it evokes. To remain there, however, means finally a surrender to hate. Those who, like the unmerciful servant, cannot let go of the debt owed by another necessarily give their lives over to anger and resentment. And a life controlled by anger cannot be anything but destructive in the end; without forgiveness of the other, one loses the possibility for joy, except for the fleeting pleasure one might derive from vengeful retaliation. The cost of not forgiving, then, is even greater than the cost of forgiving.[26]

Jesus calls us to a higher way. Recognizing our own need of mercy, instructed by our own experience of God's graciousness to us, we offer the gift of forgiveness to the other. If I have known—really known—the "amazing grace of God," how can I refuse mercy to another?

From Text to Sermon: "Forgiveness Is a Two-Way Street"[27]

According to Matthew, the disciples were talking with Jesus about practicing forgiveness in community controversies.

Peter asked, "Lord, if another member of the church sins against me, how often should I forgive? As many as seven times?" (Matt 18:21). The world is cluttered with church divisions and splinter groups because people have been unwilling to forgive even once!

Jesus turned to Peter and replied, "Not seven times, but seventy-seven times." Of course, Jesus is making the point that if one is keeping score there probably is no forgiveness in the first place.

The discussion undoubtedly left the disciples wide-eyed. Jesus then proceeded to tell a parable about forgiveness and the lack of it. He said that the realm of heaven is like a king who in settling accounts with his servants discovered one who owed him millions of dollars. He ordered the liquidation of all the servant's assets, including the sale into slavery of the man and his whole family. The servant got down on his knees and begged for patience—for just a little more time. The king not only relented; he even forgave the entire debt!

As the forgiven servant left the palace, he encountered a fellow slave who owed him what amounted to about three weeks' wages. He grabbed his debtor by the throat and demanded immediate payment. The debtor fell down on his knees and pleaded for more time. But the one whom the king had forgiven refused to show mercy. He ordered the man to be thrown into the debtors' prison.

This episode disturbed the other servants, who therefore reported it to the king. He summoned the forgiven servant and ordered that he be tortured until he had paid the entire debt. At the end of the parable, Jesus delivered the punch line: "So my heavenly Father will also do to every one of you, if you do not forgive your brother or sister from your heart."

What a shattering remark! God does not forgive us if we do not forgive others. Jesus made this plain, also, when he gave his disciples a model for praying. The only phrase that he amplified was the one about forgiveness: " . . . if you do not forgive others [their trespasses], neither will your Father forgive your trespasses" (Matt 6:14).

In other words, the slandering of the Holy Spirit—the ultimate rejection of God—is not the only unforgivable sin! The other is the ultimate rejection of another person, the refusal to forgive.

Shakespeare has moving lines about forgiveness in the court scene in "The Merchant of Venice," where Portia says to Shylock:

> The quality of mercy is not strain'd,
> It droppeth as the gentle rain from heaven
> Upon the place beneath: it is twice blest;
> It blesseth him that gives and him that takes:
> 'Tis mightiest in the mightiest; it becomes
> The throned monarch better than his crown. . . .[28]

How then do we explain the action of our "throned monarch"? Is God vindictive and cruel? Does God punish out of spite because we do not forgive those who have wronged us?

Of course not! The crux of the problem is not that God is not *willing* to forgive, but rather that God *cannot*—I repeat, *cannot*—forgive us if we do not have the spirit of forgiveness in our hearts. The refusal to forgive means the rejection of another person. The door that is slammed in the face of that person is slammed in the face of God. Christ cannot enter, for he stands with the person who is rejected. The writer of 1 John puts it this way: "Those who say, 'I love God,' and hate their brothers or sisters, are liars; for those who do not love a brother or sister whom they have seen, cannot love God whom they have not seen" (1 John 4:20 NRSV).

The refusal to forgive is a poison which neutralizes the power in the chemistry of love. A life filled with hate—in this case, the lack of forgiveness—has no room for God's love. No room for God's forgiveness.

Although the grace of forgiveness is qualitative rather than quantitative, Jesus in the parable of the unforgiving servant contrasts a debt of millions of dollars owed to the king, on the one hand, to a relatively small debt owed by the man's fellow servant. Who of us could compare the wrongs afflicted upon us with the burden of our sin for which Christ died?[29] Among twentieth-century readers, as among those who first heard this parable, are those who may be blind to their own sins and fret only about personal hurts.

John Wesley on one occasion was trying to intercede with Governor George Oglethorpe in behalf of a servant who had gotten into the governor's wine and drunk the contents of several bottles. The governor said, "Sir, I never forgive." Wesley replied, "Then, I hope you never offend."

The cost of withholding mercy is great. If, as in the lines from Shakespeare, mercy is "twice blest," it is equally true that refusing to forgive is twice cursed. Indeed, the curse is triple-fold. The lack of forgiveness hurts the person who is not forgiven. It hurts the person who refuses to forgive. And it grieves God. Mercy, like electricity, must have full circuit: from God to me, from me to my neighbor, and from my neighbor back to God.

The tragedy of the church is that so often it mouths God's mercy but fails miserably in its own practice. We forget that the church is the society of the forgiven. My sin, when I confess it, is what lets me into the church, not what keeps me out. Forgiveness is not an elective, it is a compulsory course. It is mercy or death—the death of love, the death of the human spirit.

George Bernard Shaw once wrote, "Forgiveness is a beggar's refuge . . . we must pay our debts."[30] If Shaw is indicting those who try to dodge their responsibilities, we agree. Forgiveness is not softness or sentimentality. It does not wink at wrongs or condone hurts. As Dietrich Bonhoeffer has put it so well, grace is a free gift, but it is not cheap.[31] To forgive is expensive. After all, in the parable it costs the king millions of dollars! In a legend about the parable of the prodigal son, the prodigal is pictured as coming back home in the evening. He learns the cost of his father's forgiveness only the next morning, when in the daylight he sees that his father's hair has turned completely white. Above all, we see the cost of forgiveness when we look at the cross.

> See, from his head, his hands, his feet,
> Sorrow and love flow mingled down:
> Did e'er such love and sorrow meet,
> Or thorns compose so rich a crown?[32]

Yes, to forgive is expensive. The refusal to forgive, however, costs even more. It embitters the life of the one who withholds mercy. If we could go merrily on our way by withholding mercy and cherishing our grudges, then we might escape the due consequences. But we cannot. The unforgiven wrong festers within us until the health of the soul is affected and all of life is tainted.

There is a legend about Leonardo da Vinci's painting, "The Last Supper." He is said to have painted the likeness of an enemy when he painted the face of Judas. Later, when he tried to paint the face of Christ, he could not succeed. Troubled in spirit, he blotted out the face of Judas and forgave his enemy. Then the spirit of da Vinci was set free to paint the portrait of Christ. Only when we forgive another shall we discover that the blindness of our hearts is removed and we are enabled to see God.

The pragmatists among us would want a word to be said about the difference between forgiveness and the consequences of wrongs forgiven. Forgiveness does not mean that society will not demand punishment for misdemeanors and felonies. Forgiveness does not mean that an abused spouse is forced to stay in an unbearable relationship. The victim of AIDS may forgive the one who infected him or her, but that mercy given and received does not arrest the course of the disease. Forgiveness may remove the bitterness in a broken relationship, but it may not mend a marriage. A person recently divorced said to me, "My ex-husband and I are still good friends." Forgiveness is an attitude, a spirit, an act. It may dissolve the bitterness, but it does not obviate all the consequences of wrongs and hurts.

Again, we see the offense of judgment. Justice runs its course. Punishment may be part of the toll. Mercy intercedes, but the bills keep rolling in. Even resurrection from the dead failed to remove the marks in the hands and feet of the one who was crucified.

Only God, in forgiving, also forgets. Don't find fault with the one who says, "I can forgive, but I can't forget." Forgiveness removes the arrow, yet the scar remains. Yes, the scar remains, but the wound is healed. And here we see the miracle of grace as well as the offense of judgment.

If it is true, as Jesus said, "Blessed are the merciful, for they will receive mercy" (Matt 5:7), then the corollary must also be true: "Cursed are the unforgiving, for they shall not be forgiven." Who said that Christianity is easy?

A Postscript

Some persons preaching on the parable of the unforgiving servant may wish to touch on the problems faced by those who cannot forgive themselves. Would Peter, who denied his Lord, and Paul, who persecuted the Lord's disciples, have become the great apostles of the first-century church, if beyond God's mercy they had not forgiven themselves? We wonder how the story of Judas might have been written if he had known and accepted the grace available.

For Further Reading

Donahue, *Gospel in Parable*, 72–79.
Meier, *Matthew*, 206–09.
Schweizer, *Good News according to Matthew*, 375–79.
Scott, *Hear Then the Parable*, 267–80.

WEALTH: BARRIER TO BLISS? THE PARABLE OF THE RICH MAN AND LAZARUS (LUKE 16:19–31)

In the gospels, Jesus has much to say on the subject of wealth. The cost of discipleship (the theme of our ch. 2) means, among other things, a willingness to let go of one's wealth. Jesus warns potential disciples that they must say no to their possessions if they want to follow him (e.g., Luke 14:33). And he shocks a rich inquirer by challenging him to give away all his wealth and follow Jesus (Mark 10:17–31 and par. in Matt 19:16–30; Luke 18:18–30). The practice of almsgiving (extending help to the needy) had long been an important expression of Jewish piety. Jesus clearly endorses that tradition of self-giving for the benefit of others, yet he also radicalizes the demand. Wealth, it seems, poses an obstacle to discipleship, an imposing barrier blocking entrance into the realm of God.

The Gospel of Luke is especially "rich" in passages addressing the theme of wealth, and in this gospel the dangers of wealth come into sharp focus. In addition to the texts already mentioned (14:33; 18:18–30), one thinks of the parable about a rich fool in 12:16–21. Here, a successful farmer decides to tear down his storage barns in order to make room for an especially abundant harvest. He has it made; his future is secure. He can now relax and celebrate. Nevertheless, the wealthy farmer overlooked one thing, his mortality, and on that very night he dies. The parable implies that the rich man was foolish because his world was too small. There was only room in it for one person and his needs and his security—while the hunger of needy persons in the community probably went unnoticed. What good is all that accumulated wealth now?

One also thinks of the vivid parable contrasting the fortunes of a rich man and a poor beggar (Luke 16:19–31). In fact, this entire chapter of Luke revolves around the question of the appropriate use of possessions (consider also the parable of the dishonest manager and related sayings in 16:1–13, a passage we will discuss in the next chapter).[33] This challenging parable of "rich man, poor man" casts in bold relief the question: Does wealth represent an insurmountable barrier to heavenly bliss?

Translation

There was a rich man, and he was dressed in purple and fine linen and everyday feasted sumptuously. Now lying at his gate was a poor man named Lazarus, who was covered with sores, and he longed to have his stomach filled with the food that fell from the rich man's table. But instead the dogs would come and lick his sores.

Yet it happened that the poor man died and was carried by the angels to the bosom of Abraham, while the rich man also died, and he was buried. In Hades, as he was in torment, he lifted his eyes and saw Abraham far away, and in his bosom Lazarus. He called out, "Father Abraham, have mercy on me, and send Lazarus to dip the tip of his finger in water and cool off my tongue; for I am in agony in this flame." Abraham, however, said, "Child, remember that you received your good things during your lifetime, while Lazarus dur-

*ing his lifetime received bad things. But now he receives comfort
here, and you are in agony. Moreover, a great chasm has been
placed between us and you, so that those who want to cross over to
you from here are not able, nor can one cross from there to us."*

*But [the rich man] said, "Then I ask you, father, to send him to
the house of my father—for I have five brothers—to give them
warning, so that they may not also come to this place of torment."
Abraham, though, replied, "They have Moses and the prophets; let
[your brothers] listen to them." But he said, "No, father Abraham,
if someone goes to them from the dead they will repent." He said to
him, "If they do not listen to Moses and the prophets, they will not
be convinced even if someone rises from the dead."*

An Interpretation

This is a story about reversal. It turns on the stark contrast between the fortunes of two men in this life, and in the
afterlife. A rich man descends from a life of comfort to the
experience of unrelieved torment, while the poor man ascends
from a life of misery to enjoy the company of "father Abraham." The story enacts dramatically the beatitude and woe
earlier spoken by Jesus: "Blessed are you who are poor, for
yours is the kingdom of God. . . . But woe to you who are rich,
for you have received your consolation" (Luke 6:20, 24).

This parable is noteworthy as the only extant parable of
Jesus that names any of its characters. Abraham, in Jewish
memory the founding patriarch of the nation, symbolizes here
the consolation and communion of God's realm (cf. the imagery of feasting with Abraham, Isaac, and Jacob in Matt 8:11).
The poor man, who though silent and passive throughout the
story is its central character, bears the significant name Lazarus,
meaning "God is my help."[34] As the story unfolds, it is clear
that Lazarus will receive no help from other people; his only
hope rests in the kindness of God.

The rich man and Lazarus live in close proximity; the
poor man lies on the rich man's doorstep. And yet their worlds
are light-years apart. The one man leads a life of conspicuous
consumption and great pleasure. The images of his luxurious
lifestyle are graphic: expensive purple clothing and ample
feasts day after day. In a social system that assumed that there

was a finite amount of wealth which must be distributed among all the people (a limited-goods economy), the lifestyle of the rich man would be regarded as an affront to other, less fortunate members of the community. Of course, beyond the simple fact of his wealth and his life of luxury, we do not know much about this rich man. Was he a good husband and father? Was he honest in his business dealings? Did he faithfully fulfill his religious obligations? The parable is silent about such matters—except, that is, for the one great religious obligation the man disavows. The symbol of his moral failure is his evident refusal to extend a helping hand—or even a few crumbs—to the poor beggar whom he must pass every day when he leaves his home. At his death, the wealthy man receives an honorable burial.

Lazarus, on the other hand, is truly destitute. He lies (literally, "has been thrown") at the rich man's gate, where he waits in vain to be nourished by the surplus from feast after bountiful feast. As he lies, helpless and powerless, dogs even make a meal of him, licking his sores. He has lived in misery, and dies unmourned—without, we may surmise from the narrator's silence, the benefit of burial (v. 22).

After death, however, the two men exchange places. Comfort now comes to the afflicted, and affliction to the comfortable. Though still a member of Abraham's family,[35] the rich man is now beyond even compassionate Abraham's reach. Abraham explains, "You received your good things during your lifetime . . . . " Is the rich man judged simply for being wealthy? The juxtaposition, both here and throughout the parable, of the rich man and Lazarus suggests that it is not wealth alone that condemns the man to eternal misery. Rather, his fault lies in his neglect of the needy man at his doorstep, in his blind pursuit of a life of luxury in full view of a destitute man whom he will not lift a finger to aid. In fact, nothing changes after death. The rich man still cannot see Lazarus as a person of worth. No, he is a slave to be sent to relieve the rich man's pain, or to warn his brothers. Faced with the sobering truth in post-mortem judgment, the rich man, absorbed with his own need, still cannot understand. Since Moses and the prophets had already taught the supreme importance of acts of kindness and compassion for the benefit of the needy, the rich man and his brothers are without excuse. If they have lived their whole lives oblivious to the expectations of Moses and the prophets, not even a visit from the realm of the dead will convince them that God really does want people to love their neighbors.

The parable of the rich man and Lazarus pictures God (through the voice of Abraham) as siding with the poor and broken. Judgment therefore comes to those who live only for themselves and refuse to share their resources with the poor. Once more, grace and judgment are intertwined, but this time they take aim at different targets. Grace finally reaches the poor beggar, while judgment at long last settles the score with the rich man clothed in purple. The challenge this parable addresses to the reader, then, is to act in a way the rich man would not, that is, to be an instrument of the offer of divine grace to those in need. To judge from the stakes defined by the story, this is not one option among others. It is what God expects of all who have experienced the bounty of divine grace.

We might have selected other passages in which Jesus sounds the chord of divine judgment, or, viewed from the other side, that of human accountability. Perhaps, though, enough has been said to suggest a helpful interpretive approach to these texts. Jesus' message of the "offense of judgment" places him squarely within Israel's prophetic tradition. We who hear these words need to answer for the way we respond to the extravagant grace of God. The depth of our commitment to the ways of heaven—to mercy and justice and compassion—is serious business.

From Text to Sermon: "What a Burden: To Be Rich!" [36]

Jesus pulled no punches when he talked about our stewardship of all of life: our possessions, our native abilities, our time, our neighbors. He continually challenged people who were wealthy. He said that money could make the entrance into God's realm so narrow that a camel more easily could pass through the eye of a needle (Matt 19:23–24). He told a story about a rich farmer whose self-centered plans out-ran the time he presumed to have before his sudden death (Luke 12:16–21). It could be said of that rich man what the noted television journalist, John Chancellor, observed recently in the light of his battle for health: "Cancer underscores your mortality—it's a reminder of how short a leash you're on. As I read somewhere, 'You want to make God laugh? Tell him your plans.' "[37]

The issue vividly confronts us in Jesus' parable of the rich man and Lazarus. He portrayed a man so rich that he wore expensive tailor-made robes and daily feasted on gourmet meals. Every day, a poor man was dropped by his friends at the rich man's gate. He was too ill to work and longed to eat the bread that the rich man's guests used, like napkins, to wipe their hands and mouths and then hurled into the trash. The ulcers on the poor man's body were irritated and infected by the wild dogs that licked the sores. (Unlike our view of dogs today, in Jesus' time dogs were considered "unclean.")

The rich man died and went into the torment of Hades. The poor man also died and was carried by the angels to the bosom of Abraham. Jesus used the post-mortem imagery familiar to his listeners. Hades was for the rich man a place of severe discomfort. Paradise (as we may call Abraham's bosom) for the poor man was an experience of comfort and bliss. In his torment the rich man begged Abraham to send Lazarus, like a slave, to cool his tongue with water. Abraham countered that the great gulf between Hades and Paradise prevented passage back and forth. The rich man then pleaded to have Lazarus raised and return to earth to warn the rich man's brothers lest they, too, end down in Hades. He argued, "They will listen to someone raised from the dead." Abraham, though, replied, "No, they have the Law and the Prophets as their Bible. If they don't listen to them, they won't heed even a person raised from the dead."

So the parable leaves the rich man in Hades, tortured, shall we say, by his belated regrets and a conscience that burns with an unrelieved sense of guilt. On the other hand, the parable leaves Lazarus in the realm of bliss.

Why did the rich man go to Hades? Simply because he was rich? No! Because he was indifferent! He knew Lazarus' name and he did not have him forcibly removed from his gate. But he never really saw him. For him Lazarus was merely part of the landscape. Why did Lazarus go to Paradise? Simply because he was poor? No! Because he was poor in spirit! Lazarus is the only person given a name (other than Abraham here) in all of the parables of Jesus. And what a name! The name means, "God is my help." (From Jerome's Latin version of the Bible we also learn why the rich man is called in some translations "Dives." The Latin word for "rich" is *dives*.)

Jesus was using imagery and symbolism familiar to his readers. They are not the point of the story, but they do show us what the parable implies about the afterlife. (1) When people die, they retain their personal identity. What makes you "you" and me "me" has continuity between life on earth and what comes after we die. (2) Also, death becomes the great leveler and equalizer: the rich man does not take his wealth with him, and Lazarus leaves his poverty and sickness behind. The injustice—so obvious in the contradiction between the rich man's enjoyment of this life and the poor man's suffering—is finally reversed. (3) Death does not obliterate memory: the rich man has full recall. In fact, after death probably the only things that fade into oblivion are troubles and forgiven sin. (4) People recognize one another: the rich man recognizes Lazarus and Abraham. We shall call each other by name, and as the apostle Paul remarks, then "we will see face to face" (1 Cor 13:12). I heard one man say that when he dies he feels sure that he will recognize and be surprised to see certain people in Paradise. Then he added, "I probably shall note the look of surprise on some people's faces when they recognize and see me there!"

Let us hasten, however, to dwell on the point of the parable. The rich man filled his life with everything money could buy, and he lived in luxury. His wealth probably was gained honestly. Possibly he gave to the Jerusalem "United Way." He may have headed the board of Judea's "Salvation Army." He may have been named one time "Citizen of the Year." He undoubtedly entertained in his palatial home the most prominent people of the whole region. Yet he suffered from this fatal flaw: he had no time or place for personal compassion and individual concern. He was blatantly indifferent. If he ever noticed Lazarus, it was only to regret that the man was too ill and weak to be his slave. The rich man's money was not tainted, but in his lack of compassion for individuals in need, the use of his money was wasteful and irresponsible.

God allows some people to have more money, more talent, more ability, so that they may take on *greater responsibility*. To be so blessed is to be called into greater stewardship.

Recently the *Ladies' Home Journal* carried an article written by Jim Jerome after his interview of Kathy Lee Gifford, for many years the co-host with Regis Philbin on the television program "Live." Her husband, Frank Gifford, is a well-known sportscaster and former football star. The two of them are quite wealthy. In the course of the interview, she said, "I am not here on earth to amass riches. . . . If God has blessed Frank and me with riches, it is because He knows we will not hoard them or do harm with them, but share them."[38]

Stewardship calls for sharing and serving. It makes our lives a good Samaritan's journey on the Jericho roads of our community and churches. Recently at a Rotary Club meeting, I heard a member promote a new program with the statement, "This does not require our money. This is a 'hands-on' project." On a regular basis former President and Mrs. Jimmy Carter involve themselves personally in one of the Habitat for Humanity projects. They put on overalls and help with the hammer and saw to build homes for needy families. Faithful stewards personalize their commitments and involvements. They may choose anonymity for themselves, but they put "names" on their beneficiaries! They see the Lazaruses of their neighborhood and are not indifferent to their hurts and cries for help.

The tragedy of the "Dives" types of the world is put unforgettably in the lines by G. A. Studdert-Kennedy:

> When Jesus came to Golgotha they hanged Him on a tree,
> They drave great nails through hands and feet, and made a
>   Calvary;
> They crowned Him with a crown of thorns, red were his
>   wounds and deep,

For those were crude and cruel days, and human flesh was
    cheap.
When Jesus came to Birmingham, they simply passed Him by,
They never hurt a hair of Him, they only let Him die;
For men had grown more tender, and they would not give Him
    pain,
They only just passed down the street, and left Him in the rain,
Still Jesus cried, "Forgive them, for they know not what they
    do,"
And still it rained the winter rain that drenched Him through
    and through;
The crowds went home and left the streets without a soul to see,
And Jesus crouched against a wall and cried for Calvary.[39]

Studdert-Kennedy titled this poem "Indifference."

And indifference and coldness of heart are called into judgment by the parable about the rich man and Lazarus. Yet we can experience the grace, the grace of Jesus Christ, when we come to Lazarus in our time and place. When we come to Lazarus, we shall always find Jesus there also.

For Further Reading

Donahue, *Gospel in Parable*, 169–80.

Fitzmyer, *Gospel according to Luke*, 2.1124–36.

Luke Timothy Johnson, *The Gospel of Luke* (SP 3; Collegeville, Minn.: Liturgical, 1991) 249–57.

Marshall, *Commentary on Luke*, 632–39.

Halvor Moxnes, *The Economy of the Kingdom: Social Conflict and Economic Relations in Luke's Gospel* (OBT; Philadelphia: Fortress, 1988) 139–50.

Scott, *Hear Then the Parable*, 141–59.

ENDNOTES

[1] Literally, "the sons of men [people]."

[2] In this context, the Greek word *blasphēmiai* is perhaps better translated "slanders" than "blasphemies," for the issue is hostile criticism of Jesus' healing ministry. Nevertheless, the nuance of "profaning the holy" is also very much in view, as Jesus' critics label demonic the

activity of *God.* Moreover, one should not miss the way in which Jesus now turns the tables on his opponents, who have previously accused him of speaking blasphemy (when he claimed authority to pronounce sins forgiven, Mark 2:5–7).

[3] Matthew, too, draws a sharp contrast between speaking against Jesus, the Son of humanity, and speaking against the Holy Spirit (12:32). Only the latter act is beyond forgiveness.

[4] A point made also by Meier, *Matthew,* 135.

[5] Cf. Schweizer, *Good News according to Mark,* 86.

[6] One might call a sermon based on this text "This Dangerous Freedom," or "Playing with Fire."

[7] William M. Clow, *The Cross in Christian Experience* (New York: Hodder & Stoughton, 1908) 28.

[8] *The Interpreter's Bible* (New York/Nashville: Abingdon Cokesbury, 1952) 7.693.

[9] Ibid.

[10] Also in the noncanonical *Gospel of Thomas* (saying 64), in a version much closer to Luke's than to Matthew's. In typical fashion, the *Gospel of Thomas* bends the parable in a direction that advocates detachment from the affairs of this world.

[11] The wedding garment in Matthew's telling of the parable is a piece of allegorical symbolism. What is at issue here is not proper attire but a moral and just life (clothing as metaphor of a manner of living). That is, the parable reinforces a prominent theme in Matthew's gospel: while the church (like the world) is a mixed company comprising both good and bad, ultimately God will separate the two, casting out the wicked (see, e.g., the parables of the wheat and tares and the good and bad fish in Matthew 13). In the scene of the wedding banquet, the point is that it is not enough to find oneself at the feast. One must dress (i.e., act, live) the part.

[12] Even if one considers the excuses legitimate, the logic of the parable is that *under the circumstances* the guests have excused themselves from a *far more important occasion.*

[13] When in the course of Christian history the parable came to be read as an allegory of the church's mission to "Jews first [i.e., those first invited], and then gentiles [guests who take their place]," it could be and was used to justify forcible conversion to Christian religion. After all, did the host not instruct the servant to "compel them to come in"? This regrettable misreading of the parable illustrates how important it is to anchor one's interpretation in the cultural realities of Jesus' world, and in that culture such an order makes perfect sense.

[14] *Lubbock Avalanche-Journal,* p. 6A, March 10, 1995.

[15] See especially Gal 3:28.

[16] In *The World's Best-Loved Poems,* compiled by James Gilchrist Lawson (New York/London: Harper & Brothers, 1927) 144.

[17] The use of the historical present verb here is striking. In this way, the narrator (Jesus) lends immediacy to the story; the hearer is "right there" for this crucial climactic dialogue.

[18] Ten thousand was the largest unit in counting, and a talent was the largest unit of currency (see Meier, *Matthew*, 208; Joachim Jeremias, *Rediscovering the Parables*, 164). This is the monetary equivalent of the "seventy-seven times" in 18:22. That is, it is an inconceivably large debt, scarcely more imaginable to the social elite than to an audience of peasants.

[19] The modern reader needs to be reminded that in the ancient Roman world well-educated and skilled slaves could rise to positions of great wealth and power, even as slaves. Of course, most slaves were not so fortunate.

[20] Precisely the kind of unnecessary detail that Jesus invariably omits from his parables, in order to rivet our attention on the key issues.

[21] The gesture that accompanies the demand for payment betrays the character of the forgiven slave and anticipates the outcome of the story: he seizes his fellow slave by the throat ("he began to choke him").

[22] One customarily invited to a banquet only those persons who could be expected to reciprocate. Jesus subverts this approach to guest lists in Luke 14:12–14, when he advises that we invite to meals those who cannot invite us in return.

[23] So the parable challenges from yet another direction our inclination to set limits on the obligation to forgive (cf. Peter's question in v. 21).

[24] Schweizer, *Good News according to Matthew*, 379.

[25] The parable application provided by Matthew in v. 35 ("So my heavenly Father will also do to every one of you . . . .") reinforces the connection between the king in the story and God. Matthew thereby underscores the parable's appeal to the reader with a sharp warning about what is at stake. This is one of the curious ironies of Matthew's gospel. The very gospel that so often summons readers to be merciful (e.g., 9:13; 12:7; 18:10–14, 21–35; 23:23) also employs menacing images of divine judgment to *motivate* mercy.

[26] This is not to say that one who is being victimized in an abusive relationship should simply go on forgiving and continue to play the part of victim. Neither the abuser nor the victim is helped by such an empty gesture of forgiveness. If the pattern of abuse persists, then one simply needs to leave. At a much later point in one's life, *after* one has some distance from the abuse and has dealt with the fear and anger, one may be in a position to forgive.

[27] One might also entitle the sermon "The Other Unforgivable Sin," or "What Costs More than Forgiveness?"

[28] "The Merchant of Venice," in *The Complete Works of Shakespeare* (ed. William George Clark and William Aldis Wright; New York: Grosset & Dunlop, 1911), Act IV, Scene 1, line 184.

[29] Cf. Robert H. Gundry, *Matthew: A Commentary on His Literary and Theological Art* (Grand Rapids: Eerdmans, 1982) 374–75.

[30] This line is spoken by Cusins in Act III of the play "Major Barbara" (vol. 3 of George Bernard Shaw, *Collected Plays with Their Prefaces* [New York: Dodd, Mead & Co., 1971] 178).

[31] See Bonhoeffer's discussion of "costly grace" in *The Cost of Discipleship* (rev. ed.; New York: Macmillan, 1959) 35–47.

[32] These familiar lines come from Sir Isaac Watts, "When I Survey the Wondrous Cross."

[33] I gladly acknowledge the stimulus given my own reflections on Luke 16 by the dissertation of my Union Seminary doctoral student Duck-ho Oh.

[34] Lazarus is a shortened form of the name Eliezer, meaning "God is my help." It is perhaps no accident that Eliezer is mentioned in Gen 15:2–3 as the slave and apparent heir of Abraham (before the birth of Isaac).

[35] The rich man addresses Abraham as "father," and Abraham in turn calls the rich man "child."

[36] A sermon based on this passage might carry one of the following titles: "Rich Man, Poor Man"; "The Road to Hell Is Paved with Cold Indifference"; "The Trouble with Having Money"; or "A Parable of Post-Mortems."

[37] *People Weekly*, January 23, 1995, 79.

[38] *Ladies' Home Journal*, April 1995, 172.

[39] G. A. Studdert-Kennedy, "Indifference," in *The Treasury of Christian Poetry*, compiled by Lorraine Eitel, et al. (Old Tappan, N.J.: Fleming H. Revell, 1982) 127.

A JESUS HARD TO UNDERSTAND: TWO ELUSIVE PARABLES

Do you not understand this parable?
Then how will you understand all
the parables? (Mark 4:13)

MANY WORDS OF JESUS ARE DIFFICULT FOR CONTEMPORARY READERS to understand because of the considerable distance standing between us and the voice of Jesus. His was a language different from our own; in fact, his own native language (Aramaic) differed from that of the New Testament gospels (Greek). When anyone's speech undergoes the inevitable transformations accompanying translation into foreign vocabulary and idioms (in this case from Aramaic to Greek, then to our modern languages), then a certain difficulty of comprehension—in some instances, irreducible—is to be expected. To some degree, we are able to close the language gap separating us from Jesus, and our own discussion of Jesus' sayings to this point has used those linguistic tools. But a person's language is an embodiment of his or her culture, and Jesus' culture was likewise not our own. Nevertheless, we can learn a great deal about the culture that Jesus knew. Here, too, we have tried to illuminate hard words of Jesus by holding them up to the light of our present knowledge of Jewish life in Palestine during the first part of the first century CE.

For all these difficulties of interpretation, it is striking that in the preceding chapters we have wrestled with sayings of Jesus that are not so much hard to understand as hard to accept, hard to "swallow," statements that for one reason or another are a source of provocation or offense. Sometimes Jesus' sayings were especially "hard" precisely because they were so easy to understand—easy to hear but far from easy to heed.

There remain, however, sayings of Jesus that are simply difficult to comprehend for modern readers. In this chapter we probe two parables whose meaning is particularly elusive for modern readers. We consider first the parable of the "dishonest manager" (Luke 16:1–8a), then turn to the parable about "help at midnight" (Luke 11:5–8).

HONESTLY NOW! IN PRAISE OF A DISHONEST MANAGER? (LUKE 16:1–8a)

No parable of Jesus has proved more obscure than the story in Luke 16:1–8 that revolves around the predicament and desperate survival tactics of a household steward who stands accused of mismanagement—whether through incompetence or dishonesty, or both.

Translation

> There was once a rich man who had a steward,[1] and the accusation came to him that this [steward] was squandering[2] his possessions. And summoning him, he said, "What is this I hear about you? Submit the account of your stewardship, for you are no longer able to serve as steward."
>
> And the steward said to himself, "What will I do since my master is taking the position of steward away from me? I am not strong enough to dig. I am ashamed to beg. I know what I will do, so that when I am removed from the position of steward, they will receive me into their houses."
>
> And when he had summoned each of his own master's debtors, he said to the first, "How much do you owe my master?" And he said, "a hundred baths of olive oil."[3] And he said, "Take your note, sit down quickly, and write 'fifty.'" Then he said to another, "And how much do you owe?" And he said, "a hundred kors of wheat."[4] He says to him, "Take your note and write 'eighty.'"
>
> And the master praised the unrighteous steward[5] because he had acted shrewdly.

An Interpretation

This enigmatic parable about a rich man and his steward confronts the interpreter with challenges at every turn. Has the steward been falsely accused? What is the meaning of the reduction in the debts? Above all, why does the master praise the steward?

An even more basic problem, however, concerns the scope of the parable. Where does the story end? Some scholars, convinced that it is not the *kyrios* ("lord" or "master") of the story but rather Jesus (the "Lord") who commends the steward in v. 8, argue that the parable ends at v. 7.[6] Such a solution eliminates, to be sure, the problem of explaining how the master could praise his dishonest manager. Yet it leaves the story without an ending; the interaction between master and manager at the start of the parable calls for a comparable scene at the end.[7] Others have suggested that the parable concludes with v. 8b ("for the children of this age are more shrewd in dealing with their own generation than are the children of light").[8] Since v. 9 begins with the formula "And I tell you," the parable would seem to include the whole of vv. 1–8, while vv. 9–13 attach to the parable further sayings of Jesus that comment on or apply the message in the story. On closer inspection, however, the language used in v. 8b seems to suit not the master in the story but Jesus.[9] The sayings of comment and application begin already in v. 8b, with the keywords "shrewdly"—"more shrewd" forming the link between parable (vv. 1–8a) and comment/application (vv. 8b–13). It is best, therefore, to regard the parable as ending with the master's praise of his "unjust steward."[10]

The crux of the parable, then, is the meaning of the steward's actions. How are we to evaluate his character? How can the master praise a dishonest steward who has cheated him out of so much capital? To some scholars, the parable reads like a "trickster tale": a rogue succeeds in duping his master. Jesus playfully invites his audience to go on a "moral holiday" at the master's expense.[11] So one gets comic relief from the "dead seriousness" which marks so much of Jesus' message. Humor was no doubt a significant feature of Jesus' speech (one need recall only the humorous image of a camel gliding through a needle's eye!). But before giving up on the parable of the dishonest manager, we ought to try again to discern in it a constructive message—all the more since its picture of a time of testing and crisis suggests that something important is at stake.

Other scholars insist that the key is to reconsider our negative evaluation of the steward. Actually, if we place the story in its cultural context, this manager turns out to be deserving of his master's praise. The rehabilitation of the steward might proceed in this way. One may question, first of all, whether in fact the steward deserves to be dismissed. He is accused, and the master abruptly fires him. True, the master demands that he produce his account book; however, this is not to investigate the merits of the charge but to take these accounts out of the steward's hands. He has already been dismissed! But are these charges fair? The verb used here—*dieblēthē* ("he was accused")—may suggest that these are slanderous charges (this verb is related to the noun *diabolos*, "devil").[12] This scene reflects badly not on the manager but on his boss.

Now out of a job, what is the manager to do? This is a moment of deep crisis for him (and, one may assume, for his family). Realist that he is, the steward knows that he is not strong enough to support himself through physical labor; neither is he willing to shame himself by becoming a beggar. Then a survival strategy occurs to him. As steward, he had handled a number of loans that are still outstanding. Of course, according to the custom of the day, he had enlarged the principal of these debts to include a substantial commission for himself (that is, after all, how he earned a living). Likely he also included in the principal the sizable loan interest that would come to his master.[13] It *had* to be considered as principal, since the law of Moses made interest ("usury") illegal. Now he decides to reduce these debts by the amount of his commission, and perhaps by the interest amount as well. He is sure to win new friends who will admire his honesty and generosity and perhaps wish to hire him to manage their affairs. His former boss can only praise him for his brilliant strategy. The steward has saved himself by foregoing the commissions to which he was entitled, and if he has cost the master anything, that was illegal gain anyway.

This approach to the parable is intriguing, and certainly has the merit of anchoring the story in the cultural world of Jesus. Yet there are difficulties. This explanation finds the key to the parable between the lines of the text in unspoken cultural assumptions supposedly held by the audience—a precarious move to make. Moreover, certain details in the parable paint the steward in an unfavorable light. If his motives are noble and he is simply removing from the debt either his own commission and/or (unlawful) interest included in the debt principal, then why the urgent direction, "Sit down *quickly* and write . . . "? And why does the narrator, in the very line in which the master commends the manager, call him an "unjust [or dishonest] steward" if in fact he is so scrupulously honest?[14] No, this approach to the parable sanitizes it, and robs it of the very moral offense that allows it to interest and challenge the hearer.[15]

We need to revisit the parable. What are we to make of this master and his steward? Our perception of the master is transformed as the story unfolds. He is first introduced to us as "a [certain] rich man" (v. 1), a label that already predisposes us to view him in a negative light (cf. the rich fool in Luke 12:16–20 and the rich man who neglects a poor beggar in Luke 16:19–31). His first action appears to confirm this initial impression. Informed (by whom we do not know) of the mismanagement of his property by his household manager, he abruptly terminates the man and demands that he surrender the accounts. It seems that this rich man is intent on turning someone *into* a beggar. Yet notice what happens when we next meet the master. Faced with the discovery that his steward has reduced several debts owed him (again, we do not know how the information came to him), he defies our expectation. With not a harsh word, he simply commends the man for his clever stratagem. As with God's realm, so too in this down-to-earth tale, grace can be found in surprising places!

Nevertheless, the central figure in the parable is the steward, not his boss, and the message of the parable surely turns

on his crisis and the way he responds to it.[16] What exactly does
he do, and how are his actions praiseworthy? It is of course
possible that the steward reduces the debts by the amount of his
commission or the loan interest.[17] Yet the parable never mentions either, so perhaps it is well not to make this the key to the
story—especially since the urgency behind the steward's movements (v. 6: "sit quickly and write . . . ") leads one to suspect
that all is not above board here. "How much do you owe my
master? Cut that in half! Trim this by a fifth!" What is the
meaning of these transactions?

Evidently word of the steward's predicament is not yet
public knowledge, and if that is true, the debtors will assume
that the steward is acting, as always, with the full authorization
of the owner. The steward, in fact, has created a situation in
which both he and his boss gain honor and admiration in the
town. What a splendid display of kindness and generosity from
the rich man and from the one charged with the management
of his extensive properties! The debtors will overflow with
gratitude, and the town as a whole will sit up and take notice of
such an extraordinary gesture on the part of one of its leading
citizens. We recall that honor in the community is an especially
prized commodity in this culture. To the public eye, then, the
steward has done nothing wrong or dishonest. Indeed, his role
in the debt "inventory reduction" has surely won him favorable
notice. He has cast himself in the part of a Robin Hood,
redistributing wealth from the very rich to the less wealthy.[18] So
he secures his future by doing more of what he was accused of
doing in the first place—dispersing the rich owner's possessions.[19] More to the point, the steward has created a new kind
of indebtedness. Now the master's debtors *owe him*. Given the
crucial importance of reciprocal obligation in the culture, the
desperate manager has indeed won friends for himself. Because
of his key role in the reduction of these loans, he has secured
his future. He will not go wanting for some time to come.

The strategy would unravel, naturally, if the master ex-
posed his steward's dishonesty. But he cannot expose his fired
manager without turning his own honor to shame.[20] How will
the community (not to mention the debtors) react if he rein-

states the full amount of these loans? The rich man's most important capital—the high esteem in which the town now holds him—will at a stroke evaporate. He will now be resented and despised. Clearly, his hands are tied. Both he and the steward know it. So all the master can do is praise his manager for a brilliant plan.

The parable pictures a man who faces a sudden and severe crisis. His future and the security of his family are at stake. He takes stock of the situation, concocts a shrewd scheme, and acts decisively to assure his survival. Is the steward, then, a model of faithful stewardship, an example of how one ought to handle financial affairs? Of course not. The series of sayings that follow the parable—with the contrast they draw between faithful and dishonest use of the "unrighteous mammon" (i.e., money)—steer the reader away from that misunderstanding (vv. 8b–13).

Rather, we have in this parable another "lesser-to-greater" argument, with logic not unlike that in the parable of the unjust judge (Luke 18:1–8) or that in the parable of the midnight visitor, to be discussed next. If this desperate steward acts shrewdly and decisively to ensure his survival, *how much more* should we react wisely to the crisis looming before us! That is, Jesus points to the crisis in human life provoked by the appearance of God's reign. Not mere survival but salvation is at stake, and if we may judge not only from this parable but also from so many other sayings of Jesus, the way we handle money is a crucial dimension of our response to the claim of God's realm. In the parable the steward solves his money problem not by dealing directly with his master but through his relationships with the debtors. The implication is that we "settle our accounts" with God through actions—responsible and generous actions—toward others. Therefore, even if the steward's conduct does not call for duplication at every point, perhaps it is not, after all, a bad idea to "make friends" through our *honest* use of *our own* wealth. And that means, in this connection, dispersing our wealth for the benefit of the needy. In the end, when we are dismissed from this life and called to account for our stewardship, perhaps we too will be surprised—despite our own mistakes and failures—to hear our Master's praise.

From Text to Sermon: "Praise for a Dishonest Manager?"

Jesus' story of the dishonest steward—the manager of a rich man's business enterprises—would in real life have made headlines in the Jerusalem *Gazette* or the Capernaum *Courier*. The steward was squandering his master's assets; he was allowing the man's wealth to be frittered away. At least this was the information that came to the rich man's attention. He apparently did not receive a satisfactory answer when he asked the steward about these rumors.

This kind of dishonest conduct makes today's headlines as well. Recently the United Way organization and the National Association for the Advancement of Colored People experienced the same kind of management crises and released those held responsible for the alleged dishonesty and mismanagement of funds.

In the parable of Jesus, the steward was called on the carpet and told to bring in the books for a full financial report. His wealthy employer told him that he was fired and ordered him to show all the figures.

The wasteful steward was at first inclined to panic. Not only had he embezzled funds; he had squandered all the money. Where could he go? What could he live on? What work could he obtain? He was too proud to beg. He was not qualified for any kind of job—even digging ditches.

Then he hit upon a plan. He would go to the rich man's debtors and cancel up to half of their obligations. For instance, a man who owed one hundred measures of oil would have his debt reduced to fifty measures. The steward said to himself, "These debtors will be so grateful to me that they will take me into their homes and give me room and board."

When the rich employer discovered what the steward had done, he commended him for his shrewdness. Possibly the boss realized that he must honor the write-offs lest he lose the respect and esteem in which he was held by his debtors, who may have assumed that the steward was acting on the boss's orders. The master undoubtedly said under his breath, "He is a crook, but what a clever rascal!"

Jesus added, " . . . the children of this age are more shrewd in dealing with their own generation than are the children of light."

Countless people, including biblical scholars, have been puzzled by this parable and the fact that it is attributed to Jesus. Would Jesus make such a scalawag a hero? Of course not. Jesus did not commend the man's dishonesty. Or his squandering habits. Or his embezzlement of funds. Jesus did not conclude that the steward won back his job. The only good thing about him was his shrewdness. He was, as George Buttrick described him, a rascal and a rogue.[21] Caught in the web of his own corrupt and irresponsible actions, he still found a way to save his own neck.

Luke quoted Jesus, in what may have been our Lord's comments originally spoken on other occasions, with several timely observations: If a person can't be trusted with a penny, don't trust him with a million dollars. If a person squanders money, "the unrighteous mammon," who will entrust to that one the "true riches," that is, the treasures of God's realm? And if a person does not serve faithfully as the steward for someone else, how will he or she be a steward for his or her own talents and treasures?

It seems to me, however, that the main point of the parable is found in these words: "And I tell you, make friends for yourselves by means of unrighteous mammon, so that when it fails they may receive you into the eternal habitations" (v. 9 RSV). Money, in the hands of the dishonest steward, was what he used to "buy" himself some friends, who gave him bed and board. Money is nothing in itself. It is simply the medium of exchange by which a person obtains something he or she needs or wants. Jesus is saying to us, "Take your money and translate it into things of true value, things which last, things which bless, things which take on eternal significance." Thus, money can be baptized into acts of love and deeds of mercy.

A man who was once wealthy but lost almost everything in a series of financial setbacks was visited by a friend. As they walked through the house, the friend noticed on one wall the picture of a mission complex (chapel, school, and hospital) for which the man had in more prosperous times given the money. He said to his friend, "This is one of my intangible assets."

Every time we give to or serve some worthy cause or help some needy person, we are exchanging money or energy for what has eternal value. Not that we are buying our way into heaven. Rather, we simply discover one of the principles on which God has fashioned the operation of the universe. Jesus put it this way: " . . . give, and it will be given to you. A good measure, pressed down, shaken together, running over, will be put into your lap; for the measure you give will be the measure you get back" (Luke 6:38 NRSV).

We note the urgency with which the dishonest steward, when his mismanagement came to light, began to act. It behooves us to analyze our own stewardship before God and take steps to correct our failures. Have we been squandering God's creation? The prophet Malachi announced God's indictment of those who were cheating on their tithe (3:8–12). They were, in fact, robbing God. We are prone to forget that God is the owner of all things. Nothing belongs finally or completely to us. We are the stewards, the managers. Are we not also embezzlers of God's world and its treasures? Do we not misuse, mismanage, fritter them away? In this sense, perhaps, Jesus intended for us to identify God with the rich man in the parable. From the parables of the talents (Matt 25:14–30) and of the pounds (Luke 19:12–27) we note that stewards are held accountable. There *is* a day of reckoning.

The stories of two well-known men may help us to see both the earthly and the eternal sides of stewardship. Think of the life of Alfred Nobel.[22] One morning in 1888 Nobel picked up a French newspaper and was shocked to see his own obituary. An error by a French news reporter had resulted in an article about the death of Alfred Nobel. (Actually, his brother had died.) In this story Nobel saw himself as the world saw him: "the dynamite king." He was the industrialist who had made his fortune by manufacturing and selling explosives. Nobel's passion for a peaceful world received no mention in the obituary. From that very day Alfred Nobel began to arrange for the disposition of his estate, with instructions to establish in his name the prize to be given to the person or persons who had done the most for the cause of world peace. The "unrighteous mammon" in the form of dynamite was translated into something eternal: the cause of peace.

The other modern story is seen in the life of the late world-renowned violinist Fritz Kreisler. It troubled him that he received vast sums of money for his concerts. He felt unworthy of such rewards and acclaim, for he felt that his musical talent was a gift from God. With the help and supervision of his wife, Kreisler began to give his money to worthy causes. He sometimes gave concerts *gratis* in order to raise money for a charitable organization. In fact, his biographer estimates that Kreisler gave away more money than any other artist of all time.[23] One could say that he qualified for the divine friendship which receives people into the "eternal habitations."

Is this not the point of the parable and the secret of being a good steward: translating time and talent and treasure into deeds which have an earthly touch, but also have an eternal significance? Just as a parable is an earthly story with a heavenly meaning, so stewardship moves us from earthiness to eternity.

For Further Reading

Breech, *Silence of Jesus*, 101–13.
Donahue, *Gospel in Parable*, 162–69.
Fitzmyer, *Gospel according to Luke*, 2.1094–1104.
Johnson, *Gospel of Luke*, 243–49.
Marshall, *Commentary on Luke*, 614–22.
Scott, *Hear Then the Parable*, 255–66.

HELP AT MIDNIGHT (LUKE 11:5–8)

If the parable of the dishonest steward is, by common consent, among the most difficult sayings of Jesus, the parable about a friend's desperate plea for help at midnight seems, at first glance, to be quite straightforward. After all, it revolves around basic cultural values that form the "glue" of virtually every society and remain important today: friendship and hospitality. Yet there is more here than meets the eye; even such a deceptively simple story proves to be elusive.

Translation

> Imagine this: one of you has a friend,[24] and you go to him in the middle of the night and say to him, "Friend, loan me three loaves of bread, for my friend has come to me on a journey and I do not have anything to set before him." And that person will answer from inside, "Don't bother me! The door is already shut, and my children are with me in bed. I cannot get up to give [it] to you."
>
> I tell you, even if he will not get up and give to him because he is his friend, assuredly because of his shamelessness [i.e., the concern of the man inside to avoid shame] he will arise and give him whatever he needs.

An Interpretation

Considerable cultural distance stands between modern readers of this parable and its first hearers. In a day when hospitality is a much rarer virtue, we would be inclined to fault neither the host nor his neighbor for declining these requests. Jesus and his audience, however, would have regarded the neighbor's obligation and behavior as self-evident. Nobody would evade such an urgent request for aid. The momentary inconvenience of a roused sleeper pales in comparison with the pivotal community values of friendship, hospitality, and honor on which this story turns.

The host is obligated to extend hospitality to his guest, even if he has arrived late at night. The claim of hospitality is all the more compelling because the guest is also, in the words of the host, "my friend." Likewise, the neighbor must help his friend to extend hospitality. Failure to act will, in either case, bring one shame in the community. Given the crucial importance of public honor in this culture, one will act, at whatever cost in personal inconvenience, to meet the obligations of friendship and hospitality.

The central place of honor and shame in the story has been obscured by the nearly universal practice of translating

the word *anaideian* in v. 8 as "importunity" or "persistence."
With such a rendering, the neighbor is seen as responding to
the petitioner's desperate situation, or to his repeated pleas for
help, much as in the parable about a persistent widow (Luke
18:2–5).[25] The word cannot, however, bear either meaning;
rather, it has to do with the pivotal cultural value of "shame."
One characterized by *anaideia* is "shameless," or better, is
"lacking in shame."[26] In our parable, the narrator (Jesus) assumes that even a "bad" neighbor will act in a such a way as to
avoid shame. Even if the motive is not friendship but a desire to
be "shame-free," the neighbor will respond to the needs of the
man knocking at the door. Indeed, by choosing friendship and
hospitality, both men will avoid shame and win honor for
themselves—and at the minimal cost of a few loaves of bread
and interrupted sleep.

Luke places the parable in a context that is dominated by
the theme of prayer. Luke 11:1–4 presents the "Lord's Prayer" as
a model prayer to be used by the disciples. Like the parable of
the midnight caller, this prayer addresses the request for bread
(*arton*)—though each day, rather than "in the middle of the
night." This model prayer urges a directness and simplicity in
petitionary approach to God ("give us bread," "forgive us our
sins"). The verses following the parable pick up this thread,
with their astonishing picture of a God who will withhold no
good gift from the one who petitions: "Ask, and it will be given
to you; seek, and you will find; knock, and it will be opened for
you" (11:9 our translation).[27]

How does this narrative context illuminate the message
of the parable? In the story Jesus tells, even a reluctant neighbor can be counted on to respond when a friend needs help.
How much more can we rely upon the gracious God to meet
our needs—with the gift of the Holy Spirit, no less (v. 13)! As
in the parable of the dishonest steward (and also in the much
closer parallel, the parable of the widow and the unjust judge
[Luke 18:2–5]), the logic of the parable takes the form of
a lesser-to-greater argument. If an unscrupulous judge will
surely assist a widow who persists in her quest for justice, how
much more certain is God's help for the faithful who cry out

for vindication. If even a bad neighbor comes to one's rescue in order to save face, we may with so much greater confidence bring our prayers to a loving God who stands ready to give us what we need before we ask.

The parable, then, teaches a lesson on prayer, but even more a lesson on the nature of faith. Capitalizing on crucial social norms of hospitality, friendship, and honor, Jesus sketches a picture of bold trust, born out of desperate need. Do we dare to entrust ourselves so completely to God? Now *that* is where this saying of Jesus becomes truly difficult!

From Text to Sermon: "The Prayer of Desperation (The Parable of the Midnight Caller)"

Prayer was a vital part of Jesus' life. Luke's gospel gives special prominence to this feature of Jesus' ministry. According to Luke, when the disciples on one occasion heard their Master pray, they said, "Lord, teach us to pray" (Luke 11:1). They knew the prayers they had memorized in their synagogue education. They had heard the prayers of the overly pious which were uttered on the street corners. But they sensed something different about the way in which Jesus prayed, and so they asked Jesus to teach them to pray. He proceeded to give them a model, which we commonly call "The Lord's Prayer" (or the "Our Father"). Then he told them a story. A man was surprised one night by the late arrival of a friend. Such a guest—regardless of the hour—would expect to be given food and drink to refresh him after his journey.

We are reminded of the kind of hospitality that was shown to travelers in America's frontier days. Strangers, as well as friends, who showed up at one's door were invited to share a meal and to "stay the night." In the parable of Jesus, the host was expected to provide such hospitality. He had this problem, however: his pantry was completely empty! The hour was late—midnight—but he ran over to his neighbor's house and kept hammering on the door until he awakened his friend, who was in bed with his family. If he gets up, he will disturb the whole household. But not only is the needy neighbor his friend; his refusal to provide the requested three loaves of bread would be a breach of community custom and honor. Shame would come crashing down around his head if people should learn that he had defied the time-honored rules of neighborliness. Beyond even the tug and pull of friendship for his neighbor, his fear of public shame prompted him to "get up and give him whatever he needs."

Jesus presses home the point of the parable: How much more will God respond to the needs of those who pray. God will give good things to those who ask. God will do even more than this; he will give himself (the Holy Spirit). God's generous love, then, may be contrasted to the grudging assistance of a friend.

> A weathercock that once placed
> A farmer's barn above,
> Bore on it by its owner's will
> The sentence, "God is love."
>
> His neighbor passing questioned him,
> He deemed the legend strange—
> "Now, dost thou think that, like the vane,
> God's love can lightly change?"
>
> The farmer smiling shook his head,
> "Nay, friend, 'tis meant to show
> That God is love, whichever way
> The wind may chance to blow."[28]

Jesus' parable of the midnight guest contrasts God's unchanging love to the whims and wiles of inconstant people like ourselves.

This story is prefaced, as we have seen, by the request of the disciples that Jesus teach them to pray. Luke introduces the parable about a widow and an unscrupulous judge (Luke 18:2-5) as being "about their need to pray always and not to lose heart." The first point we make is this: *Prayer is not an option; it is a necessity.* It is like the beating of the heart or like breathing. Prayer is the breath of the soul. It is water for the thirsty spirit. It is bread for the hungering heart.

Tennyson wrote in "Morte D'Arthur":

> More things are wrought by prayer
> Than this world dreams of. Wherefore, let thy voice
> Rise like a fountain for me night and day.

For what are men better than sheep or goats
That nourish a blind life within the brain,
If, knowing God, they lift not hands of prayer
Both for themselves and those who call them friend?
For so the whole round earth is every way
Bound by gold chains about the feet of God.[29]

Richard J. Foster gave his book on prayer the subtitle, "Finding the Heart's True Home."[30] Surveys consistently indicate that more than nine people in ten admit that at one time or another they have prayed. And no wonder! For prayer is the bridge between earth and heaven. It is the language that people and angels use, for it is God's language. Prayer finally is not shrouded in mystery or bound by special words; it does not require a fancy vocabulary. The sigh we sigh, the wish we wish, the cry we cry, the thought we think—these are the stuff of prayer. In the words of James Montgomery:

Prayer is the soul's sincere desire,
Unuttered or unexpressed;
The motion of a hidden fire
That trembles in the breast.

Prayer is the burden of a sigh,
The falling of a tear;
The upward glancing of an eye,
When none but God is near.[31]

No, prayer is not an option; it is a necessity. For only in prayer does the soul touch the hem of heaven's garments.

In the second place, *God is not offended by either the attitude of boldness or the cry of desperation.* God listens to us in life's normalcies, but also heeds our cries in life's extremities. The pounding on the neighbor's door at midnight and the request for three loaves may seem audacious. The widow's cries day and night for vindication before a judge who neither fears God nor regards any person may seem risky and rash. Both tested the limits of human patience. Jesus implies, however, that God responds to the cries of God's children with far greater eagerness and more speedy vindication. God is more ready to answer than we are to ask.

We can feel free to take "everything to God in prayer." Nothing big enough to worry about is too small to pray about. A farmer once heard a little orphan boy repeating the letters of the alphabet over and over again as he knelt on the hard, stony ground near the farmer's house. "What are you doing, lad?" the farmer asked. "I am praying," replied the child. "But that's not praying," the man answered. The boy said, "Yes, sir, I know it's not, but, you see, I don't know how to pray, and I heard the minister say that if a person talked to God, God would know what that person needed most. I thought I would just say the letters of the alphabet and let God put them together into the kind of prayer that I would like to say."[32] This is not too far from the meaning of the apostle Paul when he reassures us that "we do not know how to pray as we ought, but the Spirit himself intercedes for us with sighs too deep for words" (Rom 8:26 RSV).

> Have we trials and temptations?
> Is there trouble anywhere?
> We should never be discouraged:
> Take it to the Lord in prayer![33]

In the third place, *be persistent! Keep on praying!* After the parable of the midnight caller, Luke adds these words of Jesus (11:9 our translation): "And I tell you, Ask, and it will be given to you; seek, and you will find; knock, and it will be opened for you. For everyone who asks receives, and the one who seeks finds, and for the one who knocks it will be opened." Most of our English translations miss the full import of Jesus' words. A more accurate translation would be: "Keep on asking . . . keep on seeking . . . keep on knocking." Be persistent. Don't lose heart. Don't give up.

The Bible provides us with many examples of faith's per-severance. Abraham persisted in his intercession for the welfare of his nephew, Lot, and his family, when it became known that Sodom and Gomorrah would be destroyed. Abraham, the "friend of God," pleaded with God to spare the city if it contained fifty righteous persons—or only forty-five, or forty, or thirty, or twenty, or even as few as ten (Gen 18:22–23). The apostle Paul tells us that three times he prayed that his "thorn in the flesh" (whatever it was) might be removed (2 Cor 12:8). And Jesus in the Garden of Gethsemane prayed three times about the "cup" that was before him (Matt 26:44).

Do we persist because we are attempting to twist God's arm or to overcome reluctance on God's part? No! We keep on praying so that we may come to know assuredly that what we pray for is what we really want. We keep on praying so that we may discover more clearly God's will. In other words, we pray not to change God but to change ourselves.

From these parables about a midnight caller and a persevering widow, we are inspired to see the greatness and the graciousness of God. We also find that our faith is put to the test. Jesus concludes the parable of the persevering widow and the unscrupulous judge by asking, "When the Son of humanity comes, will he find faith on the earth?" (Luke 18:8 our translation). The Son of humanity is in our midst; are we willing to entrust ourselves to such a God? And do we recognize how desperate our need is? We need the living bread. We need the gracious vindication that only the judge of the universe can offer. We are helpless without the living God. Therefore we ought "to pray always and not to lose heart."

For Further Reading

Donahue, *Gospel in Parable*, 185–87.
Fitzmyer, *Gospel according to Luke*, 2.909–13.
Marshall, *Commentary on Luke*, 462–65.
Scott, *Hear Then the Parable*, 86–92.

ENDNOTES

[1] Or manager: he has been charged with managing the rich man's financial affairs.
[2] Literally, "scattering his possessions." The same verb is used of the younger son in Luke 15:13.
[3] That is, a quite large amount, probably about 800–900 gallons. See Jeremias, *Rediscovering the Parables*, 143–44; and Fitzmyer, *Gospel according to Luke*, 2.1100.

[4] Again, a sizable debt, although we cannot be sure of its precise magnitude (two passages in the Jewish history written toward the end of the first century CE by Flavius Josephus give quite different figures for the volume of this dry measure, the kor). One hundred kors was, at minimum, one hundred bushels and perhaps ten to twelve times that quantity. See Jeremias, *Rediscovering the Parables*, 143–44; Fitzmyer, *Gospel according to Luke*, 2.1101.

[5] Literally, the "steward of unrighteousness."

[6] E.g., Joachim Jeremias, *The Parables of Jesus* (New York: Scribner's, 1972) 45–47; John Dominic Crossan, "The Servant Parables of Jesus," *Semeia* 1 (1974) 7–62.

[7] Cf. Joseph A. Fitzmyer, "The Story of the Dishonest Manager (Lk 16:1–13)," *TS* 25 (1964) 23–42, esp. 27; Scott, *Hear Then the Parable*, 256–60.

[8] This position is advanced, e.g., in the commentaries on Luke by Alfred Plummer (*The Gospel according to Luke* [5th ed.; ICC; Edinburgh: T. & T. Clark, 1922]), John M. Creed (*The Gospel according to St. Luke* [London: Macmillan, 1930]), and E. Earle Ellis (*The Gospel of Luke* [NCB; Camden, N.J./London: Thomas Nelson, 1966]).

[9] The master, that is, as the parable's narrator (Jesus) characterizes him, for in v. 8a it is the narrator who reports the master's praise of the steward. Jesus is also speaking in v. 8b, but now he gives an explanation for the master's praise of the steward (the steward embodies worldly cunning). Jesus, then, speaks in v. 8a as the narrator of the parable, and beginning in v. 8b as a commentator on the events narrated in the parable.

[10] This is the view of Scott, *Hear Then the Parable*, 256–60; Fitzmyer, *Gospel according to Luke*, 2.1094–1104; and Donahue, *Gospel in Parable*, 163.

[11] See Via, *The Parables*, 155–62 (159); cf. Crossan, "Servant Parables." Scott (*Hear Then the Parable*, 264–65) points out, though, that the parable's ending (the master's praise of the rogue) subverts the trickster tale sub-plot. Hearers can no longer delight in the rogue's duping of a master who refuses to retaliate; instead, they are forced to question their earlier negative view of the rich man.

[12] See Scott, *Hear Then the Parable*, 261. I. Howard Marshall points out, however, that while there may be hostile intent behind the accusation, the fact that steward and master alike take the charges seriously shows the accusation to be true (*Commentary on Luke*, 617).

[13] See Fitzmyer, "Story of the Dishonest Manager," 31–35; J. Duncan M. Derrett, "Fresh Light on St. Luke XVI.I: The Parable of the Unjust Steward," *NTS* 7 (1960–61) 198–219, reprinted in *Law in the New Testament* (London: Darton, Longman & Todd, 1970) 48–77. Fitzmyer sees the debt relief in terms of the steward's commission, while Derrett highlights the inclusion of interest within the loan principal.

¹⁴ One might argue that it is the steward's earlier conduct (his squandering of the master's property in the first place) that wins him the label "unjust." The steward, then, becomes just and honest in time of crisis. Yet surely the narrator's description of the steward as "unjust" or "dishonest"—coming as it does at the close of the story—refers to the debt reductions just narrated.

¹⁵ In an intriguing essay ("Jesus and the Rogue in Luke 16,1–8A: The Parable of the Unjust Steward," *RB* 96 [1989] 518–32), William Loader recognizes this moral offense but interprets it differently. Viewing the unauthorized reduction of debts as a metaphor for Jesus' offer of forgiveness, Loader regards the parable as a defense of Jesus' "rogue ministry of grace to the least deserving" (531). Jesus "tells a subversive story to topple the norms and expectations of his powerful critics. His is a roguery of divine grace which confounds the arithmetic of the righteous" (532).

¹⁶ Donahue, though (*Gospel in Parable*, 168), contends that the parable really revolves around this foolish (that is, surprisingly gracious) master.

¹⁷ If indeed they are loans rather than the share of the harvest owed the landlord by his tenant farmers, a possibility noted, e.g., by Jeremias, *Rediscovering the Parables*, 143; and Johnson, *Gospel of Luke*, 244.

¹⁸ Judging from the sizes of the loans, these debtors command considerable means themselves, though obviously much less than their wealthy creditor. If, on the other hand, they are tenant farmers, their social and economic position would be much more tenuous. Verse 5, however, does call them "debtors." Moreover, what advantage would accrue to the steward by making "friends" of poor tenant farmers?

¹⁹ An ironic twist noted by Johnson, *Gospel of Luke*, 247; cf. Mary Ann Beavis, "Ancient Slavery as an Interpretive Context for the New Testament Servant Parables with Special Reference to the Unjust Steward (Luke 16:1–8)," *JBL* 111 (1992) 37–54 (50).

²⁰ See Bailey, *Poet and Peasant*, 86–110.

²¹ George A. Buttrick, *The Parables of Jesus* (New York: Harper & Brothers, 1928) 117–28.

²² See Nicholas Halaz, *Nobel* (New York: Orion, 1959) 3–4.

²³ See Louis P. Lochner, *Fritz Kreisler* (New York: Macmillan, 1950) 85.

²⁴ It is nearly impossible to capture the structure of the Greek in a fluid English translation. Literally, the text reads: "Which of you will have a friend and will go to him in the middle of the night . . . and that one would say, 'Don't bother me . . . '?" This mini-parable takes the form of a rhetorical question, which expects a negative answer. Of course no one has a friend who would act in such a manner!

²⁵ Note the intriguing parallel between Luke 11:7 (*mē moi kopous pareche*: "Don't wear me out with blows," an idiom meaning "Don't

bother me") and Luke 18:5 (*dia ge to parechein moi kopon*: "because [this widow] is wearing me out with blow[s]").

[26] For discussion of the meaning of the word *anaideia* here, see Scott, *Hear Then the Parable*, 88–91; and J. Duncan M. Derrett, "The Friend at Midnight: Asian Ideas in the Gospel of St. Luke," in *Studies in the New Testament* (vol. 3; Leiden: Brill, 1982) 31–41. Scott argues from the structure of the parable that it is the *giver's* (the sleeper's) desire to avoid shame that is at issue, while Derrett believes it is the *asker* whose "want of shame" is featured (35–36).

[27] These are present-tense imperatives, suggesting that the asking, seeking, and knocking are not single actions but represent continuous activity (of petition).

[28] An anonymous poem, quoted in *A Treasury of Sermon Illustrations* (ed. Charles L. Wallis; Nashville: Abingdon Cokesbury, 1950) 144–45.

[29] From "Morte D'Arthur," by Alfred Lord Tennyson, printed in *Great Poems of the English Language*, compiled by Wallace Alvin Briggs (New York: Tudor, 1933) 795.

[30] Foster, *Prayer: Finding the Heart's True Home* (San Francisco: Harper, 1992).

[31] James Montgomery, "Prayer Is the Soul's Sincere Desire," in *The Hymnbook* (Richmond/Philadelphia/New York: Presbyterian Church U.S., United Presbyterian Church U.S.A., and Reformed Church in America, 1955) 331.

[32] William E. Phifer, Jr., in *The Cross and Great Living*, as quoted in *A Treasury of Great Sermon Illustrations* (ed. Charles L. Wallis; Nashville: Abingdon Cokesbury, 1940) 230.

[33] From *The Presbyterian Hymnal* (Louisville: Westminster/John Knox, 1990) 403.

THE OFFENSE OF JESUS' HUMANITY

Is this not the carpenter, the son of Mary?
(Mark 6:3)

IN THE ROCK OPERA "JESUS CHRIST SUPERSTAR," MARY MAGDALENE ponders her confusion about Jesus, who is, after all, "just a man." Indeed, modern film depictions of Jesus typically enrage many Christian viewers, who object to the all-too-human portrait of their Lord (the most recent example: Martin Scorsese's "The Last Temptation of Christ"). Twenty centuries of Christian devotion to Jesus as Lord and Son of God make a full embrace of Jesus' humanity exceedingly difficult for many today. They have been nourished in a religious tradition whose contours are defined (for example) by the Gospel of John, which sharply accents Jesus' divine origin and character;[1] the Nicene Creed, which affirms Jesus' status as "true God of true God, begotten and not made, of one being with the Father"; and the Chalcedonian formula (451 CE), which reaffirms Jesus' full divinity and humanity, while identifying inappropriate ways of understanding the relation of the divine and human "natures" in Jesus.[2]

The human figure of Jesus has receded behind the impressive divine figure of John's gospel and of subsequent Christian reflection. Many contemporary Christians may not realize the importance of the affirmation of Jesus' humanity in Christian theology. After much struggle and debate, early Christian leaders ultimately rejected the attractive "docetic" view that Jesus, as a divine savior, was not fully and authentically a man. He only appeared to be subject to the constraints—not least suffer-

ing and death—that all persons must face. Unreflective do-
cetism, in which the divine nature of Jesus overshadows his
humanness, is perhaps a dominant view in the theology of
popular North American Christianity. But is this view defensi-
ble biblically?

Several passages in the gospels reveal a very human Jesus.
These texts pose a genuine challenge for preachers and teachers
who wish to honor the best of Christian tradition but also
remain faithful to the witness of scripture. For the sake of
interpreters who wish to address this challenge head on, we
consider in this chapter problematic sayings of Jesus that high-
light the "human factor."

JESUS AND THE END OF TIME:
WAS HE MISTAKEN? (MARK 9:1; 13:30)

Sprinkled liberally throughout the gospel narratives, we discover in the teaching and preaching of Jesus various images
of the near approach of the eschatological (end-time) reign
of God. A crop ripe for harvesting, a fig tree about to bear
fruit, a storm brewing in the west, servants watching at the
door for their master's return, a desperate flight in haste to
the mountains—all these images (and more) mark the present moment as a time of urgent crisis. Jesus interprets his
exorcisms, moreover, as signs and actions of God's mighty
rule, which "has come to you" (Luke 11:20). Jesus was evidently convinced that the history of God's people had, in his
day and specifically in his own work, come to a decisive
crossroad. Life would not continue after the same old patterns; it could no longer be business as usual. The transformation of Israel's social life—and of all human life—was
underway.

Two assertions of Jesus are particularly troublesome, for
they press beyond a general tenor of urgency and imminence to
offer a rather precise chronological limit to this divine project
of transformation.

Translation

> Truly, I tell you, there are some standing here who will not taste death until they see the kingdom of God come in power. (Mark 9:1; cf. Matt 16:28; Luke 9:27)

> Truly, I tell you, this generation will not pass away before all these things [the end-time crises and deliverance described in the preceding verses] happen. (Mark 13:30; cf. Matt 24:34; Luke 21:32)

An Interpretation

These two prophetic declarations apparently locate the end-time events within the lifetime of Jesus' contemporaries (his generation). As such, the statements seem to have been disconfirmed, for history has stretched on, and we still await the promised time of redemption. Was Jesus mistaken?

There are fundamental questions here that scholars continue to debate energetically. How did Jesus view the future, and how did that expectation for the future relate to his understanding of his ministry? Some think that Jesus really did expect the end of his nation's history, and of the world itself, within a very short period of time.[3]

Others, while recognizing the importance of apocalyptic hope in Jesus' message, insist that such language about the "end" should not be taken literally. Actually, this is a vivid and dramatic way of picturing the pivotal turn the nation's history was about to take. It is about the end of an era, not the end of the world or of time itself.[4] A quite popular view these days is that Jesus' message was not eschatological at all. Far from announcing the arrival of the end of the world (or age), he affirmed the nearness of God (of God's rule) within human life. Jesus was a sage, not an apocalyptic seer. The strong interest in "eschatology" that is reflected in the gospels comes not from Jesus but from the first generation(s) of his followers.[5] Early Christian prophets, convinced after Jesus' resurrection that the end-time events were close at hand, spoke in Jesus' name prophecies such as those quoted above (Mark 9:1; 13:30). Jesus did not himself say these words.[6]

Still others have raised the discussion to a different level, employing perspectives drawn from cultural anthropology to argue that Jesus' conception of time would have been quite different from that of most modern readers. To speak of Jesus' view of the future and of its timing (or chronological limits) is misleading; Jesus, like his contemporaries, would have been thoroughly present-oriented.[7]

We cannot in the space of a few pages address all the issues that have surfaced in these ongoing debates. First, though, we venture a brief observation about the recent course of the discussion. The portrait of Jesus emerging from the work of the Jesus Seminar has a decidedly modern, or even postmodern, cast. This Jesus may continue to challenge established social convention and religious tradition (as surely the historical Jesus did), but he also becomes a teacher who is easier to hear in an age when genuinely eschatological (or millenarian) beliefs have lost intellectual credibility in many circles. But in the process Jesus is lifted out of his own place in the world, as a Jew who actually lived in 1st century Palestine under Roman occupation, when people like John the Baptizer (with whom Jesus affiliated for a time) did have concrete apocalyptic hopes. The fact that Jesus' message and ministry were framed by these strongly apocalyptic "bookends"—John the Baptizer at one end and the early Christian communities at the other—makes the attempt to paint a non-eschatological Jesus highly suspect. Yet the question of how we should *interpret* the "end-time" language and images of Jesus remains open.

So we return to the gospel accounts. We want to take seriously the presence of eschatological hope in the message and actions of Jesus; indeed, it is a constitutive feature of his work and cannot simply be deferred to the first generation of his followers. Their convictions and hopes concerning the future of Israel and of the world were, we believe, rooted in Jesus' own vision and experience of the dawning, powerfully liberating rule of God.[8]

After this long but necessary detour, therefore, we are still faced with our problem: Was Jesus in error when he spoke of the imminence of the end-time events? We need to admit at the outset that an affirmative answer to this question would not deal a devastating blow to Christian faith. The evidence of the gospels is clear: even though Jesus regularly displays remarkable powers of discernment, he does not claim to know everything. In fact, on our very subject, he says precisely the opposite. No one but God knows—Jesus himself does not know—the time of the end (Mark 13:32; cf. Matt 24:36; Acts 1:6). It is up to God and God alone to appoint the limits of the human story on earth. Jesus, then, speaks out of deep conviction about the ways of God in the world, informed by his own experience of the liberating, transforming, life-renewing power of God's Spirit in his own ministry of teaching, healing, and eating. And so the signs seem clear; God's decisive acts of restoration and judgment are imminent. But Jesus speaks with assurance and conviction, not with certitude based on divine omniscience and precognition. That would be to mix the human and divine in Jesus in a way that radically undermined his authentic humanness—that is, it would mean falling victim to one of the christological errors opposed in the Chalcedonian formula.

Jesus, therefore, could have been mistaken. But was he? Certainly some of Jesus' prophetic announcements seem to have been validated by subsequent events. Of special interest is the demise of the temple and the fall of Jerusalem, prophesied by Jesus (e.g., Mark 13:1–2 and par., with many echoes in the interrogation of Jesus after his arrest and elsewhere in the gospels) and realized in the catastrophic outcome of the Jewish rebellion against Rome (70 CE). About this "end of an era" Jesus was, it turned out, remarkably prescient. Now, if all the apocalyptic imagery used by Jesus had as its "real meaning" the issuing of a warning to his people concerning the crossroad that lay before Israel, then his assertion that "all would happen" within that generation was, one might argue, confirmed, not disconfirmed.

It seems much more likely, however, that by the "coming of the kingdom of God in power" Jesus meant much, much more than the crisis Israel experienced in the year 70 CE. There is an entire world in need of re-creation; the "gone-wrongness" of the whole of human social and political life cries out for redemption and transformation (cf. Rom 8:18–25). The God whom Jesus called "Abba" and whom Jesus pictured as compassionately engaged with the lives of all sorts of people—across all the boundaries and barriers so carefully constructed in human society[9]—would surely regard the world we know as an unfinished project. The work of God's kingdom goes on still!

In a sense, then, Jesus was mistaken. Yet the central claim in his message did not have to do with the timing of a series of events. Rather, Jesus confronted his hearers with the claim that God was already acting decisively in their midst to redefine human life and community. The evidence of God's kingdom was there to be seen, and in so many ways, in such unexpected places and faces. It could be glimpsed in the tears of forgiven "sinners." One could get a taste of it in the joy of meals celebrating the goodness of God's gift of life and of human companionship. Its potential to rekindle hope could be witnessed in lives once twisted and limited by sickness and disability but now restored to dignity and wholeness. One could feel its depth and power in the renewed commitment of many people to dedicate all of life—and at considerable risk and cost—to the service of God. In a quite tangible and decisive way, the life of God's "future" had broken into the human present, reordering human community by expanding the family of God—and thereby challenging prevailing patterns of social order and power. If Jesus believed that God would finish that work in a short time, God has nevertheless in heaven's inscrutable wisdom and patience allowed the human project that is also God's project to continue, with no end yet in sight.[10]

The work God began in the ministry of Jesus, therefore, continues among us. We answer the call to discipleship and so honor Jesus, not by gazing into the future and wondering when it will all end (cf. Luke 17:20–21; Acts 1:6–8), but by committing ourselves here and now to the joyous, compassionate, and world-changing life of the kingdom of God.

From Text to Sermon: "Was Jesus Mistaken about the Future?"

In this chapter, as we consider the offense of Jesus' humanity, we are dealing with three questions with which people wrestle as they ponder Jesus' last days, his death, and his view of the end of time. We might call a sermon series on this theme "The Humanness of Jesus," with the subtitles "1. Was He Mistaken about the Future?"; "2. Was He Afraid to Die?"; and "3. Did God Forsake Him at the Cross?"

The first heresy about the person of Jesus that occurred in the early Christian church was not doubt about his divinity but doubt about his humanity. From time to time through the centuries this same heresy has raised its head. Not everyone could be so easily satisfied as Richard Watson Gilder in his "Song of a Heathen":

> If Jesus Christ is a man—
> And only a man—I say
> That of all mankind I cleave to him,
> And to him will I cleave alway.
>
> If Jesus Christ is a God—
> And the only God—I swear
> I will follow Him through heaven and hell,
> The earth, the sea, and the air![11]

Many Christians today find it easier to accept the divinity of Christ than to accept fully his humanity. We see this, for example, in the Christmas lullaby "Away in a Manger." The anonymous author of the second stanza wrote:

> The cattle are lowing, the poor Baby wakes,
> But little Lord Jesus, no crying He makes. . . . [12]

The implication is that Jesus, unlike every other baby, did not cry. Jesus not only cried like other babies, he wept when he became a man. He wept at the grave of his friend Lazarus. He wept over the city of Jerusalem. His physical strength, like ours, had its limits. He grew tired at the end of the day. He fell asleep on a boat ride across the Galilean sea. He knew hunger and thirst. And sometimes he became angry.

Jesus was the Son of God, but he was also fully human. The writer of Hebrews had this to say about Jesus: " . . . we have not a high priest who is unable to sympathize with our weaknesses, but one who in every respect has been tempted as we are, yet without sin" (Heb 4:15 RSV). In a mystery too deep for words or full human understanding, in Jesus Christ God became the Son of humanity so that we could become through him the sons and daughters of God.

If Jesus was fully human, was his knowledge limited? While he lived on earth, did he know about electricity and radar and computers? The answer is "No." When he spoke about the things that would happen at the end of time, was he in any way mistaken? "Yes!" He said that some of his contemporaries would live to see the kingdom of God come in power and the end-time crises take place. More than nineteen hundred years have passed and these predictions have not yet been fulfilled.

We can say that some of God's plans and God's time schedule were beyond Jesus' knowledge. He said one day as he was talking about end-time events, "But about that day and hour no one knows, neither the angels of heaven, nor the Son, but only the Father" (Matt 24:36 NRSV).

We are living today in a time of crisis. Pressures of change and the incredible explosion of knowledge (*future shock*, as Alvin Toffler put it in his book of that title)[13] make life hard to manage. Computers are connected in networks that put on the screen facts and figures and messages from all over the world. In the so-called secular realm prophets of doom sound the alarm as though we are living in the last days. They talk about the destruction of the ozone layer; they predict a severe international crisis owing to the rapidly depleted sources of energy, the threat of overpopulation, and the pollution of air, water, and soil. Others (have they read 2 Pet 3:10–13?) warn against the threat of nuclear war and annihilation.

Many people are fascinated, or even fearful, about the future. Some turn to astrology and look in the daily paper to read their horoscope. Jeanne Dixon is a household name.

We are not surprised, therefore, that many Christians are taking interest in "Bible prophecy." Books like Hal Lindsey's bestseller *The Late Great Planet Earth* and Pat Robertson's *The New World Order*[14] and countless television religious programs indicate that apparently some Christian leaders think that they know more than Jesus claimed to know about the end of time.

Periodically some preacher will predict the return of Jesus on a particular day and will gather his flock on some hillside to await the climactic event. During my years of ministry in Amarillo, Texas, a faith healer came from the Northwest to conduct a revival. The nightly meetings were held in the civic center. On the last night he asked the audience how many believed that Jesus might return that very night. Almost every hand went up. The evangelist said, "You are right. And if Jesus does return tonight, you won't need a single bit of the money you have in your pocket or purse. Remember this as the ushers now pass the plates to receive the evening offering!"

That faith healer joined the long line of those who through the centuries have predicted the end.[15] All of them have been mistaken. They confirm the fact that nobody except God knows and controls the timeline and the future.

At this point, it is well to mention two things about which Scripture is quite clear. In one passage (Matt 12:38–39), some of the scribes and Pharisees said to Jesus, "Teacher, we wish to see a sign from you." Jesus answered them, "An evil and adulterous generation asks for a sign; but no sign shall be given to it except the sign of the prophet Jonah." What is the sign of Jonah? Repentance and resurrection! When Jonah preached judgment to the people of Nineveh, they repented, and God gave them life and a second chance. Out of the ashes of their repentance they "rose again." All that the Bible says about the last days is a call to repentance and new life. Our generation, too, must heed the sign of Jonah.

This story of Jonah leads us to another Scripture passage that offers a few words about Bible prophecy. The prophets of the Bible—like Isaiah, Jeremiah, Amos, and Jonah—were called by God to interpret God's word and will to their generation. Their primary emphasis was *forthtelling*: they told forth God's message for the people. They dealt with the life and issues of the people of their day. The books of Daniel and Revelation have often been misinterpreted at this point. The prophetic word in both these books was given to help the people of God come through very trying days of trouble and persecution. The same is true of all the prophets.

The minor emphasis of the prophets was *foretelling*: they sometimes foretold what the future held in store. They made predictions. They saw God's unfolding purpose and acts beyond their own day and age. The gospels tell us that Jesus identified himself with some of these prophetic visions, such as those of Isaiah and Jeremiah.

We must remember a crucial fact about this practice of foretelling. All the words of the prophets concerning God's future acts are provisional and conditional. Jonah knew this and for that very reason tried to escape God's call to preach judgment to the people of Nineveh. He hated these people and was afraid that if they repented of their sin God would not punish them.[16] This leads us at long last to the other pertinent passage to which we referred earlier. God said through the prophet Jeremiah (18:7–10 NRSV):

> At one moment I may declare concerning a nation or a kingdom that I will pluck up and break down and destroy it, but if that nation, concerning which I have spoken, turns from its evil, I will change my mind about the disaster that I intended to bring on it. And at another moment I may declare concerning a nation or a kingdom that I will build and plant it, but if it does evil in my sight, not listening to my voice, then I will change my mind about the good that I had intended to do to it.

What then about the future? Can we speak some clear word about God's plan and purpose for the people of God and for the whole world? In the vast panorama of Scripture we get a grand view of God's unfolding purpose. History ("His story") is going somewhere. It is not winding down; it will be a winding up! Evil will end through God's intervention. God's holy city (a church without blemish) will be established. The kingdom will fully come. What God has begun with the new creation in Christ will be finished.

The *Presbyterian Confession of 1967* sums up its vision of the future in these words:

> God's redeeming work in Jesus Christ embraces the whole of [human] life: social and cultural, economic and political, scientific and technological, individual and corporate. It includes [humankind's] natural environment as exploited and despoiled

by sin. It is the will of God that his purpose for human life shall be fulfilled under the rule of Christ and all evil will be banished from his creation.

Biblical visions and images of the rule of Christ such as a heavenly city, a father's home, a new heaven and earth, a marriage feast, and an unending day culminate in the image of the kingdom. The kingdom represents the triumph of God over all that resists his will and disrupts his creation. Already God's reign is present as a ferment in the world, stirring hope in [humankind] and preparing the world to receive its ultimate judgment and redemption.[17]

In the meantime we continue to put our trust in God through Jesus Christ our Lord. No one—people on earth or angels in heaven, or even Jesus himself in his life on earth—knows the time schedule. But we live by God's never-ending grace. We live day by day in the shadow of eternity. Let us be about the work of that kingdom that is among us, yet still to come in its fullness. Let us live ready to meet Jesus face to face. Let us live in hope. Let us walk by faith. Let us live in prayer.

And our prayer may well be:

Lead thou me on:
Keep thou my feet;
I do not ask to see
The distant scene—
One step enough for me.[18]

For Further Reading

Marcus J. Borg, *Jesus: A New Vision* (New York: Harper & Row, 1987).

Marcus J. Borg, *Meeting Jesus Again for the First Time: The Historical Jesus and the Heart of Contemporary Faith* (San Francisco: HarperSanFrancisco, 1993).

Raymond E. Brown, *Introduction to New Testament Christology* (New York: Paulist, 1994).

A. J. Conyers, *The End: What Jesus Really Said about the Last Things* (Downers Grove, Ill.: InterVarsity, 1995).

John Dominic Crossan, *Jesus: A Revolutionary Biography* (San Francisco: HarperSanFrancisco, 1994).

Luke T. Johnson, *The Real Jesus: The Misguided Quest for the Historical Jesus and the Truth of the Traditional Gospels* (San Francisco: HarperSanFrancisco, 1995).

Meier, *A Marginal Jew*, 2.237–506 (a detailed and rather technical discussion of the issues from a historical perspective).

Pheme Perkins, *Jesus As Teacher* (Cambridge: Cambridge University, 1990).

Ben Witherington, *Jesus, Paul, and the End of the World: A Comparative Study in New Testament Eschatology* (Downers Grove, Ill.: InterVarsity, 1992).

WAS JESUS AFRAID TO DIE?
(MARK 14:36; MATT 26:39, 42; LUKE 22:42)

Attentive readers of the Synoptic Gospels encounter a puzzling tension in each of these portrayals of Jesus. Well in advance of his arrest, on the one hand, he more than once delivers a remarkably clear and precise prediction of his approaching death at the hands of the authorities in Jerusalem (Mark 8:31; 9:31; 10:33–34; and par.). He is therefore not caught by surprise when his adversaries gain the upper hand; he even anticipates the act of betrayal on the part of one of his intimate companions (Judas Iscariot). Jesus goes so far as to interpret his coming death as a self-offering through which liberation (i.e., redemption—Mark 10:45) and forgiveness (Matt 26:28 and par.) are attained. That is to say, it is an event purposed by God, and one Jesus himself embraces.[19] And yet, on the other hand, he seems to stumble on his way to the cross. Otherwise so confident of his mission, so ready to embrace his destiny at Jerusalem, when he arrives at the crucial hour of testing in Gethsemane he evidently retreats in fear from the peril that looms before him.[20]

Translation

> *Abba, Father, all things are possible for you. Take this cup away from me. Nevertheless, [bring about] not what I want but what you [want]. (Mark 14:36)*

Father, if it is possible, let this cup pass from me; but [may it be] not as I want but as you [want]. . . . [A second time] Father, if it is not possible for this cup to pass without my drinking it, let your will be done. (Matt 26:39, 42)

Father, if you are willing, take this cup away from me; nevertheless, let your will, not mine, be done. (Luke 22:42)

An Interpretation

There are at least two difficult questions here. First, how are we to resolve this tension in the depiction of Jesus—the tension, that is, between the earlier confident predictions of his destiny and now the desire expressed in Gethsemane to avoid the hour altogether? Second, if indeed Jesus hoped to avoid the suffering and death that awaited him, how are we to make room for such a response within the life of the Son of God? Is this a posture worthy of emulation? In other words, we encounter once again the offense of Jesus' humanity.

We ought to begin, though, by observing the distinctive manner in which each of these three gospels narrates Jesus' prayer in Gethsemane.[21] In each narrative, while Jesus is summoning strength through prayer to face a moment of grave peril, the weary disciples succumb to sleep.[22] They are therefore unprepared for the test of their loyalty that will begin with the approach of the arresting party. Ultimately, Jesus accepts his destiny, while the disciples—after a futile gesture of violent resistance—panic and desert him.[23] If in Gethsemane we see Jesus engaged in a genuinely human struggle, we also witness the all too human failure of his followers.

Yet there are intriguing differences among these accounts.[24] Of particular interest here, Mark paints by far the darkest picture of the disciples' failure. In the Gethsemane scene, true to form, Mark gives the content of Jesus' prayer only once while placing greater weight on the disciples' sleep, which is mentioned three times. Matthew, on the other hand, by indicating three times (and quoting twice) the content of Jesus' petition, signals a shift in emphasis from the disciples' sleep to Jesus' prayerful submission to the divine will. Matthew also thereby indicates an advance in Jesus' petitions, from "if it is possible, let this cup pass from me," to "if it is not possible for this cup to pass without my drinking it, let your will be done." In Matthew, that is, as Jesus continues to pray, he is able to discern more clearly the course he must follow, and to align himself more completely with God's will. Unlike the other two gospels, Luke provides a single snapshot (not three) of Jesus at prayer and of the disciples asleep ("because of grief").

Though with somewhat different words, in all three gospels Jesus entreats God to remove the "cup" that he is about to drink. This is the same cup mentioned by Jesus at the last supper—the cup, that is, of his suffering, the cup filled with his blood, soon to be poured out (Mark 14:24 and par.).[25] Knowing all too well the depth of pain, degradation, and cruelty that lie before him, Jesus pauses to consider whether there is another way. In a real sense, then, Gethsemane forces Jesus to revisit the "wilderness" where he had first met a forceful challenge to his commitment to the ways of God (Matt 4:1–11 and par.). Now, though, the stakes have clearly been raised. What are we to do with Gethsemane? What does it teach us about the character of Jesus' life? How does it shape our reflection on the vocation of Jesus and our own identity as God's people?

First of all, Jesus' plea in Gethsemane eloquently expresses his full participation in the human condition.[26] There is perhaps fear and doubt here; certainly there is a desire to avoid pain and suffering. Here, no less than in the wilderness testing, Jesus faces a moment of grave crisis. If he possessed absolute certainty that his imminent death would be truly redemptive for the world and that God would vindicate him by raising him from the realm of death, then the prayer in Gethsemane would make no sense, and Jesus would be robbed of his humanity.

So what of the passion predictions earlier in the narrative? These passion and resurrection predictions have been shaped by retrospective Christian memory; they speak of Jesus' future with a confidence and clarity drawn from the certainty of the church's convictions and experiences after Easter. To be sure, they in all probability do articulate the historical Jesus' own sense of foreboding. After all, many prophets before him had met a tragic end (cf. Luke 13:34; Matt 23:34–36), and in view of the conflict his ministry had already provoked, Jesus was no doubt able to read the writing on the wall. The passion predictions, though, express that premonition with a precision and certitude that reflect early Christian memory after Good Friday and Easter.

What we glimpse in Gethsemane is the depth of the human struggle Jesus had to undergo *on the way to* that assurance after Easter. In the words of the letter to the Hebrews, "he was made complete through the things he suffered" and "he learned obedience from the things he suffered" (Heb 2:10; 5:8 our translation).

Through it all Jesus remains, to be sure, in intimate communion with God whom he calls "Father" (cf. *Abba* in Mark).[27] And out of that communion with God he is able to embrace an uncertain future. Yet the path he must walk is not an easy one; indeed, we will discover in the final section of this chapter that even the assurance of intimate communion with God ultimately must come into question.

It is clear, then, that the Gethsemane prayer shows Jesus standing in complete solidarity with other human beings who likewise experience struggle, are frightened by an uncertain future, and fall victim to cruelty and oppression. But wouldn't a more "heroic" approach to death provide a better model? Not at all; in fact, we hear an important corrective in these accounts. The words at Gethsemane emphatically reject a "cult of martyrdom" that would urge us to seek out persecution and victimization. On the contrary, Jesus' request that he be allowed to avoid the cup amounts to a ringing affirmation of the value and goodness of life.

True, those who dare to live out of the values of the household of God will often challenge the ways of Caesar's household, and the resulting conflict will sometimes exact a heavy cost. So Roman power will bring Jesus to his cross. But a commitment to justice and to the ways of heaven means also a tenacious affirmation of the desire for life.[28] Gethsemane—and with it the cross itself—attests to God's life-giving power, which does not wink at or trivialize the experience of suffering and death but also does not miraculously deliver us from them. Like Jesus, therefore, we approach our own experience of disgrace and suffering with uncertainty and apprehension, yet also—and finally—in trust. Finding strength and discernment through prayer, and also through the communion of friends and family (a fellowship denied to Jesus in his last hours), we entrust ourselves and our future to a loving, gracious God. Just so, in Gethsemane Jesus stares death in the face and at first recoils in anguish—but he then summons courage to embrace a perilous future, trusting in God, his Abba.

Of course, some may still want to ask how it is that we could know the content of Jesus' prayers at Gethsemane. After all, the disciples were sleeping. A brief word on this problem is appropriate before we leave this passage. We must admit, at the outset, that the gospel narratives do not answer such a question. They use the narrative technique of an "omniscient" narrator who can be present wherever necessary to tell the story (even reporting the thoughts of characters, as in Mark 2:6, 8; 3:2; Luke 5:22). They do not, however, explain how it is that the community of disciples came to obtain such information as the Gethsemane prayers of Jesus. (Were some disciples awake for some of the prayer? Did the risen Jesus inform them? And so on.)

Nevertheless, there must have been a reliable early tradition that Jesus approached his arrest and death at Jerusalem with reluctance and apprehension. Otherwise, the first Christians were scarcely likely to invent such a tradition, which seems to cast doubt on the courage and prophetic knowledge of Jesus. Perhaps the prayers of Gethsemane were but an intensified expression of prayers to which the disciples had listened for some time now. Perhaps the words represent the disciples' recall of the sort of thing that Jesus would have said at such a time. We cannot know. But we do know that the first followers of Jesus, and the gospel authors who preserved this memory of Jesus at prayer, regarded their Lord as a man who courageously and with dignity—a dignity achieved only through real difficulty—endured suffering, disgrace, and a cruel death.

From Text to Sermon: "Was Jesus Afraid to Die?"

We take off our shoes, for we sense that here we tread on holy ground. The hour about which Jesus had told his disciples was now at hand. On several occasions, the gospels tell us, Jesus spoke of his coming death.[29] He looked forward to the final confrontation with his opponents, and said that he surely would be put to death.

But as he clutched the ground and prayed in Gethsemane, he hoped that his Father, to whom all things were possible, might take the cup from him. Three times he made this request, and while he prayed these prayers, his disciples fell asleep.

How, then, if he prayed alone while they slept, do we know these details from Gethsemane? Mark tells us that there was a young man in the garden who narrowly escaped capture when Jesus was arrested (Mark 14:51–52). Was it Mark himself?[30] Possibly Mark had followed Jesus and his disciples from the upper room and had witnessed what took place in Gethsemane. Or it may be that those sleepy disciples in retrospect sewed together from their pieces of reminiscence the fabric of what they later sensed was a significant part of the last hours of Jesus' life. We cannot be sure how this tradition first arose.

"If you are willing," he prayed, "take this cup away from me" (Luke 22:42). Was Jesus afraid to die? He lived those last months in what seemed at times to be eager anticipation of his death. In fact, he lived his whole life in its shadow. Holman Hunt has a painting depicting the carpenter's shop of Joseph in Nazareth. He portrays a young Jesus, stripped to the waist, with arms raised above his head. The sun, as it streams through the open door, casts on the wall behind Jesus a shadow in the form of a cross. Hunt titled the painting "The Shadow of Death."[31]

When the hour drew near, was Jesus afraid to die? It would have been natural for a man in his early thirties to savor life and to resist the idea of dying—especially the idea of death on a Roman cross at the hands of both government and "church," death at the instigation of his own people and through the betrayal of one of his own disciples.

Was he afraid to die? Death on a Roman cross was a
terrible and horrifying thing. Spikes were driven through the
hands and feet. Scourging ordinarily preceded crucifixion—
and scourging was itself brutal physical torture. The fortunate
died after several hours of excruciating pain on the cross; for
the less fortunate, the suffering might stretch over two or more
days. Who would not seek to escape such a death?

Was he afraid to die? Stephen, according to Acts the first
Christian martyr, went bravely to his death, felled by the stones
hurled by enemies of Jesus and of his followers. Was he more
courageous than the one in whose name and for whose name
he died? In the years that followed, countless others died as
Stephen had.

Plato tells us that Socrates in an Athens prison cell drank
the cup of poison "without trembling or changing color or
expression."[32] In the presence of his tearful friends he raised
the cup and drank it to the last drop. He cheered them by
saying, "Be brave." Was Jesus less brave?

From what did Jesus withdraw? What was the "cup" that
troubled him? The cup was the symbol of death. The cup was his
blood. This was the cup that he had shared with his disciples in
the upper room. On that occasion he had said, "This is my blood
of the covenant, which is poured out for many for the forgiveness
of sins" (Matt 26:28 RSV). When Jesus looked into the cup, he saw
not only his own blood but the sins of the world—the sins of his
contemporaries, the sins of his enemies, the sins of his disciples
who forsook him and fled, the sins of all the ages, your and my
sins—a poisonous mixture far more lethal than the potion in the
cup of Socrates. Jesus, and he alone, could drink this cup. When
he would go to the cross he, the sinless one, would take the rap
for the sins of the world. In the words of the apostle Paul, "For
our sake [God] made him to be sin who knew no sin, so that in
him we might become the righteousness of God" (2 Cor 5:21
RSV). The cup contained the wrath of God. Now, the wrath of
God means "human rejection of divine love." The drinking of
that cup triggered the agony which accompanied the birthing of
the new creation. This was the darkness of human rebellion
which could only be overcome by divine light.

Here in Gethsemane is the foreshadowing of that moment on Calvary when Jesus cried out, "My God, my God, why have you forsaken me?" In our next section we shall deal with the implications of that cry. Here in the garden we catch a glimpse of the crash that was to take place at the crossroads in the universe when God's love met human hate, when the forces of satanic evil met the forces of divine good, when eternity invaded time and life won out over death. Coming to a head in the Gethsemane struggle was the crisis of the ages—the battle that began in another garden when Paradise was lost, the battle that was won by God in a garden with an open tomb, where Paradise was regained.

Donald Miller said of Gethsemane that we enter here upon a "deep, mysterious, and incommunicable moment in the life of Jesus. . . . We are moving in the unfathomable depths of the mystery of our redemption."[33] Raymond Brown writes of Mark's report of the prayer in Gethsemane: "Mark is presenting a moment that is both historical and eschatological. The suffering and crucifixion of Jesus are a physical trial for him but also part of a cosmic struggle."[34]

Next, we must never forget that Jesus' attempt to escape the drinking of the cup was part of his prayer to his heavenly Father. Here on his knees, with beads of sweat on his brow (which were "like great drops of blood"—Luke 22:44), he prayed. If it were not possible for God to remove the cup and still accomplish the divine will, Jesus would drink the cup. He prayed, "not my will, but yours be done." Here we sense that Jesus in his humanity did not presume to know God's will. He was willing to drink the cup and go to the cross if this was what it would require to do God's will.

What a lesson we learn here for our own seasons of prayer! We are encouraged to take everything to God in prayer. But we do well to add, "Please don't grant our request if it is against your will." God must sometimes say "No" for our own good or for the sake of God's larger purpose. If a child comes to a parent and says "Let me have the butcher knife," or "Give me the keys so I may drive the car," or "Let me try your medicine," the parent will say "No." Explanations of the "why not?" may not satisfy the youngster, but the answer still must be "No." As for children, perhaps later for us the wisdom of God's "No" will become clear.

Someone penned these lines:

I thank Thee, Lord, for mine unanswered prayers,
Unanswered save Thy quiet, kindly "Nay,"
Yet it seemed hard among my heavy cares
That bitter day.

I wanted joy; but Thou didst know for me
That sorrow was the gift I needed most,
And in its mystic depth I learned to see
The Holy Ghost.

I wanted health; but Thou didst bid me sound
The secret treasuries of pain,
And in the moans and groans my heart oft found
Thy Christ again.

I thank Thee, Lord, for these unanswered prayers,
And for Thy word, the quiet, kindly "Nay,"
'Twas Thy withholding lightened all my cares
That blessed day.[35]

We watch Jesus as he falls to the ground and prays. We are privileged to hear, as it were, his prayer: "Not what I want, Father, but what you want." We, too, kneel and there discover why Jesus was afraid to die. Far beyond physical pain, he suffered the anguish that our rebellion and alienation from God poured into his cup.

Finally, let us remember that God was there, listening to the prayer and agonizing in the ordeal of God's own Son. For the cup and the cross are engraved on the heart of God. God would have removed the cup from the lips of Jesus, but there was no other way. For "in Christ God was reconciling the world to himself" (2 Cor 5:19).

Yes, we take off our shoes. We bow our heads, and we praise God for a Savior who took the cup and transformed it into a cup of grace. "This cup stands for my blood, the blood of a new covenant. Your sins are forgiven, and the only sacrifice you need to make is the sacrifice of a broken and contrite heart."

For Further Reading

John Barton, *Love Unknown: Meditations on the Death and Resurrection of Jesus* (Louisville: Westminster/John Knox, 1990).

Raymond E. Brown, *The Death of the Messiah: From Gethsemane to the Grave: A Commentary on the Passion Narratives in the Four Gospels* (ABRL; New York: Doubleday, 1994) 1.146–234.

David Buttrick, *The Mystery of the Passion: A Homiletic Reading of the Gospel Traditions* (Minneapolis: Fortress, 1991).

Donald Senior, *The Passion of Jesus in the Gospel of Luke* (PS 3; Wilmington, Del.: Michael Glazier, 1989) 84–89.

Donald Senior, *The Passion of Jesus in the Gospel of Mark* (PS 2; Wilmington, Del.: Michael Glazier, 1984) 70–77.

Donald Senior, *The Passion of Jesus in the Gospel of Matthew* (PS 1; Wilmington, Del.: Michael Glazier, 1985) 76–83.

WERE YOU THERE (GOD) WHEN THEY CRUCIFIED MY LORD? (MARK 15:34)

In Gethsemane, as we have seen, Jesus resolves—though, to be sure, only through an anguished, wrenching struggle—to align his desires with the will of God, and so remains true to his commitment to God. Even in this dark hour he draws strength from his communion with God. In fact, to the bitter end the canonical gospels portray Jesus persisting in prayer to God. Perhaps this is clearest in Luke's gospel, where Jesus' prayers from the cross continue the pattern of his entire ministry.[36] Jesus petitions his Father to forgive his enemies, and he entrusts his spirit to the Father in the moment of death (Luke 23:34, 46).

Matthew and Mark, too, present Jesus at prayer in his darkest hour, but in these narratives Jesus' prayer does not affirm the supporting presence of God. Instead, he laments the seeming absence of God.

Translation

> [Jesus cried out in a loud voice,] My God, my God, why have you forsaken me? (Mark 15:34; Matt 27:46) [37]

An Interpretation

The heading of this final section of our study echoes, of course, the popular song "Were You There When They Crucified My Lord?" The lyrics of this song poignantly invite listeners to place themselves, as it were, at the cross of Jesus, where they may ponder the deep meaning of this event. Part of the profundity—and also the challenge—of this account is that it forces us, with Jesus, to confront the silence of God in the face of human suffering. This is also, then, the anguished question posed by Auschwitz—and by countless other tragedies in human history.

Jesus dies in torment, left utterly alone. The religious and civil authorities have branded him a dangerous criminal, and the people who earlier responded to his ministry with such enthusiasm have now left him to his fate. Even his closest friends and trusted companions have deserted him. His family evidently long since wrote him off as hopelessly deluded (see Mark 3:21); only in the Gospel of John does his mother Mary take her place at the crucifixion.[38] The cause to which Jesus committed his life—the project of God's kingdom, which entailed redrawing the maps of human community—seems to have come to nothing.

And now, most devastating of all, Jesus feels the loss of the most precious of resources. Abba, the divine Father, is no longer close at hand to support him. Overcome with the experience of God's distance, where else would Jesus turn to express his lament than to the scriptures? So Jesus addresses his complaint to God using the words of the righteous sufferer in Ps 22:1.

Psalm 22 begins with the complaint of one who suffers torment unjustly at the hand of the wicked. Scorned, mocked, and abused, he has cried out to God night and day; but God has remained silent. The psalm concludes, however, with affirmation. God can be counted on to vindicate the righteous sufferer. God will hear the cries of the afflicted (22:24); they will again receive nourishment and be satisfied (22:26). God's rule will be established, and all families of the earth will worship God (22:27–28).[39] Maybe Jesus has the content of the entire psalm in mind when he cries out, "My God, my God, why have you forsaken me?" If that is true, then he would be voicing despair and confident hope in the same breath. Lamenting the present remoteness of God, he would at the same time be affirming God's approach to vindicate him.[40]

Naturally, we cannot read Jesus' mind as he speaks from the cross, and so we cannot rule out the possibility that Jesus found encouragement in such reflections on the whole psalm. Yet is it not significant that the words quoted from the psalm are precisely those expressing despair in the face of God's silence? It is these words that make sense of Jesus' experience. He dies in disgrace and defeat, every support stripped away. He is truly forsaken, utterly alone.[41]

We discover at the cross, therefore, a vivid and unforgettable portrait of Jesus' full humanity. He experienced life in its beauty and splendor, and death in its cruelest guise. He was one of us.

Christian memory and conviction, however, discern deep irony in the scene of Jesus' death. All is not as it seems. Precisely in the divine silence, heaven speaks a word of hope and renewal to the world. In this very real experience of the absence of God, one encounters the mystery of God's radical solidarity with human suffering. God has drawn near in order to give life to a broken world. Easter good news makes clear what Jesus did not feel and could not know in his dying hours on the cross. God was silent, but it is an eloquent silence in which we may confront the compassionate care of the Creator.

From Text to Sermon: "Did God Forsake Jesus at the Cross?"

Jesus was a man of prayer. He often withdrew to pray. So we should not be surprised to learn that he even prayed when he was on the cross. In fact, three of the seven last sayings of Jesus (as recorded in the gospels) are prayers. The fateful hour of which he had told his disciples had arrived: "The hour is coming, indeed it has come, when you will be scattered, each one to his home, and you will leave me alone. Yet I am not alone because the Father is with me" (John 16:32 NRSV). But the unbelievable seemingly had happened. Jesus felt deserted. Where was the Father? "My God, my God, why have you forsaken me?"

This was, first of all, *the cry of aloneness.* The time comes in the life of even the most devout believer when he or she feels forsaken—and not only by loved ones and friends and neighbors, but even by God. The person of faith may well cry out in such an hour, "Why does the way of the wicked prosper?" (Jer 12:1 RSV; cf. Ps 73:3–9; Hab 1:13). A defeated Gideon asks, "If the Lord is with us, why then has all this befallen us?" (Judg 6:13 RSV). A disillusioned Job queries, "Why was I born?" (see Job 3:1–19; 10:18). A grieving father says, "Where was God when my son was killed?" Do we not find kinship with Jesus when on the cross he, too, feels forsaken?

Many years ago at a General Assembly of the former United Presbyterian Church in the U.S.A. I witnessed a play in which the only actor was a prisoner confined in a large cage made of wooden poles. The prisoner continually called out, "Hello, out there! Is anybody there?" Nothing but silence! For me it was an unforgettable parable of what it means to be alone.

Perhaps the experience that comes closest to such a moment—short of grief at the death of a loved one—is homesickness. I still have a vivid recollection of how I felt when I arrived at the seminary campus in Princeton for the first time. I had been away from home for short periods, but now I was to be away until at least the Christmas break. I ate the picnic supper my mother had packed. Every bite sent my mind speeding across the miles to my home in western Pennsylvania. I managed to eat everything in that picnic box, but when I finished I still had a strange, empty feeling in the pit of my stomach. Tears were on my cheeks, and a feeling of panic came over me. I felt alone. And I thought I could not bear it. Yet what Jesus experienced on the cross was a far greater sense of desolation.

Second, this prayer from the cross could have been *the cry of agnosticism.* Perhaps Jesus was asking simply because he could not or did not know what was taking place. Was something happening that was so profound or mysterious or puzzling that Jesus, in his limited, human knowledge, could not comprehend? Jesus had been an obedient son. He had sought always to do the Father's will. Even in the times of temptation, when his humanness was severely challenged, he had been faithful. In his hunger after forty days in the wilderness he had been tempted to reject his humanity by turning stones into bread (Matt 4:3). But he refused to do it. He had been tempted to take advantage of his Father's providential protection: "Jump from the pinnacle of the temple. Force your Father to keep you from harm" (cf. Matt 4:5–6). Again Jesus resisted. A third temptation was to compromise his kingship by trafficking with evil (Satan; see Matt 4:8–9). To do so would have been to reject the Holy Spirit. Jesus refused to compromise. Later came the temptation in Gethsemane to escape the drinking of the cup, but he overcame this temptation also. He surrendered to his Father's way: "Your will, not mine, be done." In all these trials he was tempted to risk consequences beyond his ability, as a human being, to know.

Now as he hung in the darkness on the cross, the clouds (or was it something else?) blotted out the face of God. How could he know for sure what was happening? And so the cry "My God, my God, why have you forsaken me?" could well be the cry of agnosticism.

Or, third, it could be *the cry of agony.* His hands and feet pulled against the rusty nails. His back bore the marks of the soldiers' flogging. His lips were parched with sunburn and thirst. His brow showed the open wounds from the crown of thorns which the soldiers had pressed down upon his head. He had not slept during the night because the interrogations by the chief priests and Pilate[42] had consumed the late night and early morning hours. He had been coerced to carry the cross and had collapsed under the weight of the heavy timber. He had been hanging on the cross from nine o'clock in the morning, and now it was three o'clock in the afternoon (cf. Mark 15:25, 34). The physical pain—even apart from the mental strain and spiritual struggle—was sufficient to elicit a cry of agony.

As a fourth consideration, the question flung out into the darkness—"My God, my God, why have you forsaken me?"—might very well have been *the cry of atonement.* Surely we come here to the edge, if not the very heart, of the mystery of the atonement: the way God was in Christ atoning for the sins of the world. Here Jesus drinks the cup with its deadly mixture of our rebellion against God's will and our rejection of God's love. This is the journey Jesus told the disciples he must take, with the added word, "Where I am going, you cannot follow me now" (John 13:36). This was the moment when, in the words of the Apostles' Creed, "he descended into hell." He went to hell so that we never need to go there. The battle of the ages was being waged in the invisible realms of the universe, and hints of that battle broke through here at Calvary, so that we might catch a glimpse of the cost of our redemption. In a real sense he took our place and paid the price of our freedom. What happened on the cross was the ultimate fulfillment of Isaiah's words: "Surely he has borne our griefs and carried our sorrows; yet we esteemed him stricken, smitten by God, and afflicted. But he was wounded for our transgressions, he was bruised for our iniquities; upon him was the chastisement that made us whole, and with his stripes we are healed" (Isa 53:4–5 RSV).

Arthur S. Cripps pictures the sense of isolation felt by Father Anthony as he struggles for racial justice in Africa, and compares it with Jesus' cry from the cross:

Today I sink
Into that last and deepest loneliness
Where God leaves him that has left all for God,

Where man on his own cross must taste that hell
Christ tasted once for all. For so to us
Our faith declared. But does it still declare?
Faith as all else withdraws. The night comes on.
The earthquake shatters, and from out the cleft
Creeps naked Doubt to wring her hands and wail
"My God, my God, hast Thou forsaken me?"[43]

G. A. Studdert-Kennedy penned these lines to describe what took place at Calvary:

And sitting down they watched Him there,
The soldiers did;
There, while they played with dice,
He made His sacrifice,
And died upon the cross to rid
God's world of sin.
He was a gambler, too, my Christ,
He took His life and threw
It for a world redeemed.
And ere His agony was done,
Before the westering sun went down,
Crowning that day with crimson crowns,
He knew that He had won.[44]

It was the day of atonement, and the cry of desolation was a sign that our sin came between Jesus and God. But in that moment what he had entered into our humanity to accomplish came to pass. The very forsakenness was the sign that he had won.

And if we tarry at the cross, these words "My God, my God, why have you forsaken me?" may lead us to a fifth discovery: *affirmation*. For this cry is only the beginning of a prayer that Jesus knew by heart—Psalm 22. It was a psalm that he especially could pray or sing. Beginning with this cry of desertion, its stanzas trace in a vivid way his hours on the cross: " . . . they have pierced my hands and feet . . . they divide my garments among them, and for my raiment they cast lots" (vv. 16–18 RSV). But the psalm with a great crescendo of faith also affirms the presence of God: " . . . he has not hid his face from him, but has heard, when he cried to him. . . . Posterity shall serve him; men shall tell of the Lord to the coming generation, and proclaim his deliverance to a people yet unborn, that he has wrought it" (vv. 24, 30–31 RSV). Listen with the ears of faith and you will hear the affirmation. John tells us that, at the end, Jesus cried out, *Tetelestai*, that is, "It is finished!" (John 19:30). His work on earth was done. He sensed it. And God, confirming what in Jesus' humanity he dared to hope and affirm, raised him from the dead. We have heard the rest of the story, and we accept it and affirm it. In his great name we serve. He has left the next part of the work to us. We are sent to teach and preach and heal—in his name.

> though he was in the form of God, . . .
> he emptied himself, taking the form of a servant,
> being born in human likeness.
> And being found in human form he humbled himself
> and became obedient unto death,
> even death on a cross.[45]

Let us take up our own cross each day and follow him.

For Further Reading

Barton, *Love Unknown*.
Brown, *Death of the Messiah*, 2.1043–58, 1085–88.
Buttrick, *Mystery of the Passion*.
Senior, *Passion of Jesus in Mark*, 121–26.

ENDNOTES

[1] The Gospel of John preserves, at the same time, reminders of Jesus' humanity. For example, he becomes tired (4:6) and thirsty (4:7; 19:28), he experiences grief (11:35–36) and distress (13:21), and he shows capacity for love (11:36; 13:1). When arrested, he is bound (18:12, 24) and beaten (19:1), and he finally succumbs to death (19:30, 33).

[2] For a helpful recent discussion of these christological developments, see John Macquarrie, *Jesus Christ in Modern Thought* (London: SCM, 1990) 147–72. The statement from the Council of Chalcedon affirms that Jesus is one person, "complete in Godhead and complete in manhood . . . one and the same Christ . . . recognized in two natures, *without confusion, without change*, without division, without

separation; *the distinction of natures being in no way annulled by the union*" (emphasis added; text conveniently available in Macquarrie, *Jesus Christ*, 165).

[3] A classic statement of this view is that of Albert Schweitzer, *The Quest of the Historical Jesus* (ET; New York: Macmillan, 1968; German orig. 1906). For recent treatments along this line, see Sanders, *Jesus and Judaism*, esp. pp. 152–56; and Meier, *A Marginal Jew*, 2.237–506.

[4] See, e.g., N. T. Wright, *The New Testament and the People of God* (Minneapolis: Fortress, 1992) ch. 10; and the similar approach to apocalyptic language advocated by George B. Caird, *The Language and Imagery of the Bible* (Philadelphia: Westminster, 1980) 243–71.

[5] This is the position of many members of the Jesus Seminar, a view articulated most persuasively by Marcus J. Borg in several publications (e.g., "An Orthodoxy Reconsidered: The 'End-of-the-World' Jesus," in *The Glory of Christ in the New Testament: Studies in Christology in Memory of George Bradford Caird* [ed. L. D. Hurst and N. T. Wright; Oxford: Oxford University, 1987] 207–17; and *Jesus: A New Vision* [New York: Harper & Row, 1987]); cf. also John Dominic Crossan, *The Historical Jesus: The Life of a Mediterranean Jewish Peasant* (San Francisco: Harper, 1991) e.g., 238–59.

[6] See, e.g., Borg, "Orthodoxy Reconsidered," 212–14. Meier, too (*A Marginal Jew*, 2.347–48), argues that these sayings (together with Matt 10:23) stem not from Jesus but from early Christian prophets, yet Meier concludes from other sayings that Jesus did expect the "definitive coming of God in the near future to bring the present state of things to an end and to establish his full and unimpeded rule over the world in general and Israel in particular" (2.349).

[7] E.g., Bruce Malina, "Christ and Time: Swiss or Mediterranean?" *CBQ* 51 (1989) 1–31. Malina describes the view of the "future" in ancient Mediterranean culture in these terms: "What is forthcoming stands at the concrete horizon of the present" (17). Greater and lesser remoteness (in time) from that present would not have been a consideration. Malina argues that Jesus, and New Testament authors generally, lacked a future orientation of the sort we experience; they were fundamentally "present-oriented" (29).

[8] Recall the series of images from the gospels enumerated in our discussion above.

[9] Recall the parables treated in ch. 1 above.

[10] Cf. 2 Pet 3:8–9. Of course, we have had our share of apocalyptic nightmares inspired by the nuclear umbrella under which we have lived for many decades now and, more recently, by ecological concerns.

[11] Richard Watson Gilder, "The Song of a Heathen," in *Masterpieces of Religious Verse* (ed. James Dalton Morrison; New York/Evanston: Harper & Row, 1948) 213.

[12] Quoted from *The Presbyterian Hymnal* (Louisville: Westminster/John Knox, 1990) 24.

[13] Toffler, *Future Shock* (New York: Random House, 1970).

[14] Lindsey, with C. C. Carlson, *The Late Great Planet Earth* (Grand Rapids: Zondervan, 1970); Robertson, *The New World Order* (Dallas: Word, 1991).

[15] See the fascinating study of these movements in Stephen D. O'Leary, *Arguing the Apocalypse: A Theory of Millenial Rhetoric* (Oxford/New York: Oxford University, 1994).

[16] Thereby causing Jonah twofold misery: the despised people of Nineveh would be spared, and the prophet's message of doom would appear to have been disconfirmed.

[17] The full text of the *Confession of 1967* is available in *The Book of Confessions*, Part 1 of *The Constitution of the Presbyterian Church, U.S.A.* (New York/Atlanta: Office of the General Assembly, 1983). The quoted excerpt is 9.53–54.

[18] From the first stanza of John Henry Newman's "Lead, Kindly Light," in *The Hymnbook* (Richmond/Philadelphia/New York: Presbyterian Church U.S./United Presbyterian Church U.S.A./Reformed Church in America, 1955) 281.

[19] This perspective is expressed even more emphatically in John's gospel, which highlights Jesus' sovereignty over his "hour" of death (see, e.g., John 10:17–18).

[20] Morna D. Hooker notes this tension in the narrative in her book *Not Ashamed of the Gospel: New Testament Interpretations of the Death of Christ* (Grand Rapids: Eerdmans, 1994) 61–62.

[21] John 12:27 echoes this Synoptic scene, but in a way that diminishes the depth and poignancy of Jesus' struggle to submit to the divine will: "Now my soul is troubled. And what shall I say—'Father, save me from this hour'? No, it is for this reason that I have come to this hour." John accents Jesus' equanimity, while the other gospels linger over the struggle that precedes the determined resolve.

[22] The disciples sleep out of "grief," according to Luke 22:45.

[23] Even for Peter, who bravely follows Jesus into the high priest's courtyard, the last word is a denial of Jesus born of fear (Mark 14:66–72 and par.). See the discussion of the disciples' failure in John T. Carroll and Joel B. Green, *The Death of Jesus in Early Christianity* (Peabody, Mass.: Hendrickson, 1995) 34–35; also, Donald Senior's essay on "The Death of Jesus and the Meaning of Discipleship" in the same volume (ch. 12).

[24] For a comprehensive analysis of the accounts, see Raymond E. Brown, *The Death of the Messiah: From Gethsemane to the Grave: A Commentary on the Passion Narratives in the Four Gospels* (2 vols.; ABRL; New York: Doubleday, 1994) 1.146–234.

[25] On the meaning of the "cup," see Brown, *Death of the Messiah*, 1.168–71.

[26] Senior's reflection is worth quoting: "Jesus, faithful son of God, is also a child of humanity and therefore he fears the death that threatens his mortal existence. The Gethsemane prayer is a strong antidote to any portrayal of Jesus that dilutes his humanness" (*Passion of Jesus in Matthew*, 80).

[27] Senior comments on Matthew's portrait of Jesus in Gethsemane: "Even as Jesus clutches the earth in sorrow and anguish, that deep abiding spirit of fidelity is not extinguished" (*Passion of Jesus in Matthew*, 81).

[28] Cf. Paul's reflections on this score in Phil 1:20–26.

[29] See, e.g., Mark 8:31; 9:31; 10:32–34, 45; 14:24; John 12:20–28, 32–33.

[30] We learn from Acts 12:12 that the home of John Mark's mother, Mary, was used as a meeting place by the early Christians. Was this the same person? Perhaps, though we cannot be sure. See the critical reflections in Paul J. Achtemeier, *Mark* (2d ed.; PC; Philadelphia: Fortress, 1986) 126–28.

[31] See Julian Treuherz, *Pre-Raphaelite Paintings* (Lund Humphreys, 1980). The painting hangs in the Manchester City Art Gallery in England.

[32] Plato, *Phaedo*, 117–18.

[33] Donald G. Miller, *Luke* (LBC; Atlanta: John Knox, 1959) 155.

[34] Brown, *Death of the Messiah*, 1.168.

[35] "I Thank Thee, Lord," in *The World's Best Loved Poems*, compiled by James Gilchrist Lawson (New York: Harper & Brothers, 1927) 328–29.

[36] For discussion of Jesus at prayer in Luke, see, e.g., Stephen C. Barton, *The Spirituality of the Gospels* (London: S.P.C.K., 1992) 87–91; David Crump, *Jesus the Intercessor: Prayer and Christology in Luke–Acts* (WUNT 2:49; J.C.B. Mohr [Paul Siebeck], 1992); Green, *Theology of Luke*, 58–60; Steven F. Plymale, *The Prayer Texts of Luke–Acts* (AUS 7: TR 118; New York: Peter Lang, 1991).

[37] Both Mark and Matthew give Jesus' prayer in Aramaic (with Matthew using the Hebrew form of the word "God"), then translate the complaint into Greek. The question whether the Jesus of history actually spoke these words is worth pursuing. As in the case of the Gethsemane prayer, the criterion of embarrassment strongly supports the attribution of the prayer to Jesus. Why would early Christians create for themselves such an interpretive nightmare by placing on Jesus' lips this expression of despair? For further discussion, see Brown, *Death of the Messiah*, 2.1085–88; Joel Marcus, "The Old Testament and the Death of Jesus: The Role of Scripture in the Gospel Passion Narratives," in *The Death of Jesus in Early Christianity*,

by John T. Carroll and Joel B. Green (Peabody, Mass.: Hendrickson, 1995) ch. 11.

[38] Only after Jesus has died do the Synoptic Gospels mention the presence of women, and then at a distance. Jesus' mother is not included. John, by contrast, places Mary and the other women, in the company of the beloved disciple, close to Jesus before he dies (19:25–27).

[39] Readers who know this full text of the psalm will be able to supply an answer to the question Jesus draws from v. 1. "Why [i.e., for what reason] have you forsaken me?" The reason is that God's rule may be established and proclaimed (22:31) to generations yet unborn, and that the whole world may remember, and join the chorus of praise to God.

[40] In any event, the perspective of faith after Easter has room for such affirmation; see further "From Text to Sermon" below.

[41] Hooker, too, argues that this prayer voices Jesus' despair, not the confidence expressed later in the psalm (*Not Ashamed of the Gospel*, 64–65).

[42] And, according to Luke 23:6–12, the tetrarch Herod Antipas as well.

[43] In John Robert Doyle, Jr., *Arthur Shearly Cripps* (Boston: Twayne, 1975) 33.

[44] G. A. Studdert-Kennedy, in Morrison, ed., *Masterpieces of Religious Verse*, 187.

[45] Phil 2:6–8 our translation.

SELECT BIBLIOGRAPHY

Achtemeier, Paul J. *Mark*. 2d ed. PC. Philadelphia: Fortress, 1986.

Bailey, Kenneth E. *Poet and Peasant*. Grand Rapids: Eerdmans, 1976.

_____. *Through Peasant Eyes: A Literary-Cultural Approach to the Parables of Luke*. Grand Rapids: Eerdmans, 1980.

Barth, Markus. "The Dishonest Steward and His Lord: Reflections on Luke 16:1–13." In *From Faith to Faith: Essays in Honor of Donald G. Miller on His Seventieth Birthday*. Ed. by Dikran Y. Hadidian. Pages 65–73. Pittsburgh: Pickwick, 1979.

Barton, John. *Love Unknown: Meditations on the Death and Resurrection of Jesus*. Louisville: Westminster/John Knox, 1990.

Barton, Stephen C. *The Spirituality of the Gospels*. London: S.P.C.K., 1992.

Beavis, Mary Ann. "Ancient Slavery as an Interpretive Context for the New Testament Servant Parables with Special Reference to the Unjust Steward (Luke 16:1–8)." *JBL* 111 (1992) 37–54.

Bonhoeffer, Dietrich. *The Cost of Discipleship*. Rev. ed. New York: Macmillan, 1959.

Borg, Marcus J. "An Orthodoxy Reconsidered: The 'End-of-the-World' Jesus." In *The Glory of Christ in the New Testament: Studies in Christology in Memory of George Bradford Caird*. Ed. by L. D. Hurst and N. T. Wright. Pages 207–17. Oxford: Oxford University, 1987.

_____. *Jesus: A New Vision*. New York: Harper & Row, 1987.

_____. *Meeting Jesus Again for the First Time: The Historical Jesus and the Heart of Contemporary Faith*. San Francisco: HarperSanFrancisco, 1993.

Boring, M. Eugene. "The Unforgivable Sin Logion Mark III 28–29 / Matt XII 31–32 / Luke XII 10: Formal Analysis and History of the Tradition." *NovT* 18 (1976) 258–79.

Bornkamm, Günther. *Jesus of Nazareth*. San Francisco: Harper & Row, 1960.

Breech, James. *The Silence of Jesus: The Authentic Voice of the Historical Man.* Philadelphia: Fortress, 1983.

Brown, Raymond E. *The Death of the Messiah: From Gethsemane to the Grave: A Commentary on the Passion Narratives in the Four Gospels.* 2 vols. ABRL. New York: Doubleday, 1994.

_____. *Introduction to New Testament Christology.* New York: Paulist, 1994.

Bruce, F. F. *The Hard Sayings of Jesus.* Downers Grove, Ill.: InterVarsity, 1983.

Buttrick, David. *The Mystery of the Passion: A Homiletic Reading of the Gospel Traditions.* Minneapolis: Fortress, 1991.

Buttrick, George A. *The Parables of Jesus.* New York: Harper & Brothers, 1928.

Caird, George B. *The Language and Imagery of the Bible.* Philadelphia: Westminster, 1980.

Capon, Robert Farrar. *The Parables of Grace.* Grand Rapids: Eerdmans, 1988.

_____. *The Parables of Judgment.* Grand Rapids: Eerdmans, 1989.

Carroll, John T., and Joel B. Green. *The Death of Jesus in Early Christianity.* Peabody, Mass.: Hendrickson, 1995.

Clow, William M. *The Cross in Christian Experience.* New York: Hodder & Stoughton, 1908.

Collins, Raymond F. *Divorce in the New Testament.* Collegeville, Minn.: Liturgical, 1992.

Conyers, A. J. *The End: What Jesus Really Said about the Last Things.* Downers Grove, Ill.: InterVarsity, 1995.

Craddock, Fred. *Luke.* IBC. Louisville: John Knox, 1990.

Creed, John M. *The Gospel according to St. Luke.* London: Macmillan, 1930.

Crossan, John Dominic. *The Historical Jesus: The Life of a Mediterranean Jewish Peasant.* San Francisco: Harper, 1991.

_____. *In Parables: The Challenge of the Historical Jesus.* New York: Harper & Row, 1973.

_____. *Jesus: A Revolutionary Biography.* San Francisco: HarperSanFrancisco, 1994.

_____. "The Servant Parables of Jesus." *Semeia* 1 (1974) 7–62.

Crump, David. *Jesus the Intercessor: Prayer and Christology in Luke–Acts.* WUNT 2:49. J.C.B. Mohr (Paul Siebeck), 1992.

Derrett, J. Duncan M. "Fresh Light on St. Luke XVI.I: The Parable of the Unjust Steward." *NTS* 7 (1960–61) 198–219. Reprinted in *Law in the New Testament.* Pages 48–77. London: Darton, Longman & Todd, 1970.

_____. "The Friend at Midnight: Asian Ideas in the Gospel of St. Luke." In *Studies in the New Testament*. 3.31–41. Leiden: Brill, 1982.

_____. *Law in the New Testament*. London: Darton, Longman & Todd, 1970.

_____. *Studies in the New Testament*. Vol. 3. Leiden: Brill, 1982.

Dietrich, Suzanne de. *Matthew*. LBC 16. Richmond: John Knox, 1961.

Donahue, John R. *The Gospel in Parable*. Philadelphia: Fortress, 1988.

Ellis, E. Earle. *The Gospel of Luke*. NCB. Camden, N.J./London: Thomas Nelson, 1966.

Fenton, John C. *Saint Matthew*. PNTC. New York: Penguin, 1963.

Firth, C. B. "The Parable of the Unrighteous Steward (Luke xvi.1–9)." *ExpT* 63 (1951–52) 93–95.

Fitzmyer, Joseph A. *The Gospel according to Luke*. 2 vols. AB 28–28A. Garden City, N.Y.: Doubleday, 1981–85.

_____. "The Matthean Divorce Texts and Some New Palestinian Evidence." In *To Advance the Gospel: New Testament Studies*. Pages 79–111. New York: Crossroad, 1981.

_____. "The Story of the Dishonest Manager (Lk 16:1–13)." *TS* 25 (1964) 23–42.

_____. *To Advance the Gospel: New Testament Studies*. New York: Crossroad, 1981.

Fletcher, Donald R. "The Riddle of the Unjust Steward: Is Irony the Key?" *JBL* 82 (1963) 15–30.

Furnish, Victor Paul. *The Moral Teaching of Paul*. 2d ed. Nashville: Abingdon, 1985.

Gächter, Paul. "The Parable of the Dishonest Steward after Oriental Conceptions." *CBQ* 12 (1950) 121–31.

Gibson, Margaret D. "The Parable of the Unjust Steward." *ExpT* 14 (1902–03) 334.

Green, Joel B. *The Theology of the Gospel of Luke*. NTT. Cambridge: Cambridge University, 1995.

Gundry, Robert H. *Matthew: A Commentary on His Literary and Theological Art*. Grand Rapids: Eerdmans, 1982.

Hadidian, Dikran Y., ed. *From Faith to Faith: Essays in Honor of Donald G. Miller on His Seventieth Birthday*. Pittsburgh: Pickwick, 1979.

Hare, Douglas R. A. *Matthew*. IBC. Louisville: John Knox, 1993.

Harrington, Daniel J. *The Gospel of Matthew*. SP 1. Collegeville, Minn.: Liturgical, 1991.

Harvey, A. E. *Strenuous Commands: The Ethic of Jesus*. Philadelphia: Trinity Press International, 1990.

Hengel, Martin. *The Charismatic Leader and His Followers*. Edinburgh: T. & T. Clark, 1981.

Hiers, Richard H. "Friends by Unrighteous Mammon: The Eschatological Proletariat (Luke 16:9)." *JAAR* 38 (1970) 30–36.

Hooker, Morna D. *Not Ashamed of the Gospel: New Testament Interpretations of the Death of Christ.* Grand Rapids: Eerdmans, 1994.

Hurst, L. D., and N. T. Wright, ed. *The Glory of Christ in the New Testament: Studies in Christology in Memory of George Bradford Caird.* Oxford: Oxford University, 1987.

Jeremias, Joachim. *The Parables of Jesus.* New York: Scribner's, 1972.

_____. *Rediscovering the Parables.* New York: Scribner's, 1966.

Johnson, Luke Timothy. *The Gospel of Luke.* SP 3. Collegeville, Minn.: Liturgical, 1991.

_____. *The Real Jesus: The Misguided Quest for the Historical Jesus and the Truth of the Traditional Gospels* (San Francisco: HarperSanFrancisco, 1995).

Kingsbury, Jack Dean. "On Following Jesus: The 'Eager' Scribe and the 'Reluctant' Disciple (Matthew 8.18–22)." *NTS* 34 (1988) 45–59.

Kosmala, Hans. "The Parable of the Unjust Steward in the Light of Qumran." In *Studies, Essays, and Reviews,* 2.17–24. Leiden: Brill, 1978.

_____. *Studies, Essays, and Reviews.* Volume 2. Leiden: Brill, 1978.

Lambrecht, Jan. *Once More Astonished: The Parables of Jesus.* New York: Crossroad, 1981.

Linnemann, Eta. *Jesus of the Parables.* New York: Harper & Row, 1966.

Loader, William. "Jesus and the Rogue in Luke 16,1–8A: The Parable of the Unjust Steward." *RB* 96 (1989) 518–32.

Long, Thomas G. *Preaching and the Literary Forms of the Bible.* Minneapolis: Fortress, 1989.

Long, Thomas G., and Cornelius Plantinga, Jr., ed. *A Chorus of Witnesses: Model Sermons for Today's Preacher.* Grand Rapids: Eerdmans, 1994.

Lowry, Eugene L., ed. *How to Preach a Parable: Designs for Narrative Sermons.* Nashville: Abingdon, 1989.

Lunt, Ronald G. "Expounding the Parables—The Parable of the Unjust Steward (Luke 16:1–15)." *ExpT* 77 (1965–66) 132–36.

Luz, Ulrich. *The Theology of the Gospel of Matthew.* NTT. Cambridge: Cambridge University, 1995.

Macquarrie, John. *Jesus Christ in Modern Thought.* London: SCM, 1990.

MacRae, George W. "New Testament Perspectives on Marriage and Divorce." In *Divorce and Remarriage in the Catholic Church.* Ed. by L. G. Wrenn. Pages 1–15. New York: Newman, 1973.

Malina, Bruce. "Christ and Time: Swiss or Mediterranean?" *CBQ* 51 (1989) 1–31.

Marcus, Joel. "The Old Testament and the Death of Jesus: The Role of Scripture in the Gospel Passion Narratives." In *The Death of Jesus in Early Christianity*. Ed. by John T. Carroll and Joel B. Green. Pages 205–33. Peabody, Mass.: Hendrickson, 1995.

Marshall, I. Howard. *Commentary on Luke*. NIGTC 3. Grand Rapids: Eerdmans, 1978.

McCane, Byron R. " 'Let the Dead Bury Their Own Dead': Secondary Burial and Matt 8:21–22." *HTR* 83 (1990) 31–43.

Meier, John P. *A Marginal Jew: Rethinking the Historical Jesus*. 2 vols. ABRL. Doubleday, 1991, 1994.

_____. *Matthew*. NTM 3. Wilmington, Del.: Michael Glazier, 1980.

Miller, Donald G. *Luke*. LBC 18. Atlanta: John Knox, 1959.

Moore, F. J. "The Parable of the Unjust Steward." *ATR* 47 (1965) 103–05.

Moxnes, Halvor. *The Economy of the Kingdom: Social Conflict and Economic Relations in Luke's Gospel*. OBT. Philadelphia: Fortress, 1988.

Neusner, Jacob. *The Mishnah*. New Haven: Yale University, 1988.

Oh, Duck-ho. "Faith and Wealth: A Literary-Historical Study of Luke 16." Ph.D. diss., Union Theological Seminary in Virginia, 1996.

O'Leary, Stephen D. *Arguing the Apocalypse: A Theory of Millenial Rhetoric*. Oxford/New York: Oxford University, 1994.

Parrott, Douglas M. "The Dishonest Steward (Luke 16.1–8a) and Luke's Special Parable Collection." *NTS* 37 (1991) 499–515.

Perkins, Pheme. *Hearing the Parables of Jesus*. New York: Paulist, 1981.

_____. *Jesus As Teacher*. Cambridge: Cambridge University, 1990.

Plummer, Alfred. *The Gospel according to Luke*. 5th ed. ICC. Edinburgh: T. & T. Clark, 1922.

Plymale, Steven F. *The Prayer Texts of Luke–Acts*. AUS 7: TR 118. New York: Peter Lang, 1991.

Praeder, Susan M. *The Word in Women's Worlds: Four Parables*. ZSNT. Wilmington, Del.: Michael Glazier, 1988.

Sanders, E. P. *Jesus and Judaism*. Philadelphia: Fortress, 1983.

_____. "Judaism and the Grand 'Christian' Abstractions: Love, Mercy, and Grace." *Int* 39 (1985) 357–72.

_____. *Paul and Palestinian Judaism*. Philadelphia: Fortress, 1977.

Schweizer, Eduard. *The Good News according to Luke*. Atlanta: John Knox, 1984.

_____. *The Good News according to Mark*. Atlanta: John Knox, 1970.

_____. *The Good News according to Matthew*. Atlanta: John Knox, 1975.

Scott, Bernard Brandon. *Hear Then the Parable*. Minneapolis: Fortress, 1989.

Senior, Donald. *The Passion of Jesus in the Gospel of Luke.* PS 3. Wilmington, Del.: Michael Glazier, 1989.

_____. *The Passion of Jesus in the Gospel of Mark.* PS 2. Wilmington, Del.: Michael Glazier, 1984.

_____. *The Passion of Jesus in the Gospel of Matthew.* PS 1. Wilmington, Del.: Michael Glazier, 1985.

Stambaugh, John E., and David L. Balch. *The New Testament in Its Social Environment.* LEC 2. Philadelphia: Westminster, 1986.

Stanton, Graham N. *The Gospels and Jesus.* OBS. Oxford/New York: Oxford University, 1989.

Stein, Robert H. *Difficult Passages in the New Testament: Interpreting Puzzling Texts in the Gospels and Epistles.* Grand Rapids: Baker, 1990.

Tannehill, Robert. *The Sword of His Mouth.* Philadelphia/Missoula: Fortress/Scholars, 1975.

Thielicke, Helmut. *The Waiting Father: Sermons on the Parables of Jesus.* New York: Harper & Row, 1959.

Tolbert, Mary Ann. *Perspectives on the Parables: An Approach to Multiple Interpretations.* Philadelphia: Fortress, 1979.

Topel, L. John. "On the Injustice of the Unjust Steward: Lk 16:1–13." *CBQ* 37 (1975) 216–27.

Vawter, Bruce. "The Biblical Theology of Divorce." *Proceedings of the Catholic Theological Society of America* 22 (1967) 223–43.

Via, Dan O. *The Parables: Their Literary and Existential Dimension.* Philadelphia: Fortress, 1967.

Wardlaw, Don M., ed. *Preaching Biblically: Creating Sermons in the Shape of Scripture.* Philadelphia: Westminster, 1983.

Williams, Francis E. "Is Almsgiving the Point of the 'Unjust Steward'?" *JBL* 83 (1964) 293–97.

Williamson, Lamar, Jr. *Mark.* IBC. Atlanta: John Knox, 1983.

Witherington, Ben. *Jesus, Paul, and the End of the World: A Comparative Study in New Testament Eschatology.* Downers Grove, Ill.: InterVarsity, 1992.

Wrenn, L. G., ed. *Divorce and Remarriage in the Catholic Church.* New York: Newman, 1973.

Wright, N. T. *The New Testament and the People of God.* Minneapolis: Fortress, 1992.

Wuthnow, Robert. *Acts of Compassion: Caring for Others and Helping Ourselves.* Princeton: Princeton University, 1991.

Young, Brad H. *Jesus and His Jewish Parables: Rediscovering the Roots of Jesus' Teaching.* TI. New York/Mahwah: Paulist, 1989.

INDEX OF MODERN AUTHORS

Index of Correlations to the Common Lectionary

Unforgiving servant		
Matt 18:23–35	86–95	A–24 ord.
Rich man and Lazarus		
Luke 16:19–31	95–103	C–26 ord.
Dishonest manager		
Luke 16:1–8	108–17	C–25 ord.
Help at midnight		
Luke 11:5–8	117–24	C–17 ord.
Jesus and the end of time		
Mark 9:1	129–39	
Mark 13:30		B–1 Adv.
Afraid to die?		
Mark 14:36		B–Passion
Matt 26:39, 42	139–48	A–Passion
Forsaken by God at death?		
Mark 15:34	148–55	B–Passion
Matt 27:46		A–Passion

Explanation of Symbols:

A = Year A lectionary cycle; B = Year B; C = Year C.

Each number designates a Sunday within the portion of the year indicated:

Advent	Adv.
Ordinary Time after Epiphany	ord.(E)
Lent	Lent
Palm/Passion Sunday	Passion
Ordinary Time after Pentecost	ord. (numbered in weeks after Easter).

E.g., B–1 Adv. designates the first Sunday in Advent, Year B cycle.

INDEX OF ANCIENT SOURCES